The Natural History Of The Land Of The Bible

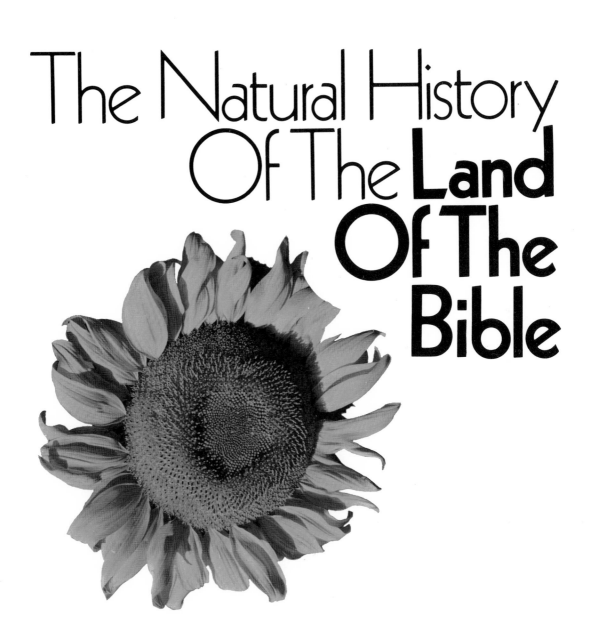

DOUBLEDAY & COMPANY, Inc.

Garden City, New York. 1978

Designed by Ziva Sivan

Assistant designer: Ofra Kamar

First published in Israel, 1969, by
G.A. The Jerusalem Publishing House Ltd.

English edition first published, 1969, by
The Hamlyn Publishing Group Limited
London - New York - Sydney - Toronto
Hamlyn House, Feltham, Middlesex, England

© Copyright 1969 by
G.A. The Jerusalem Publishing House Ltd.
© Copyright 1975 by
G.A. The Jerusalem Publishing House Ltd.
© Copyright 1978 by
G.A. The Jerusalem Publishing House Ltd.

LC 77-91916
ISBN: 0-385-14222-6

Printed in Italy by Staderini spa
Pomezia (Rome) — 1978

by Azaria Alon

CONTENTS

'A land of wheat, and barley, and vines, and fig trees, and pomegranates; a land of oil olive, and honey.'

(Deuteronomy 8:8)

left: *The olive may justly be regarded as the king of fruit trees, providing both food and oil from time immemorial to the present day.*

below left: *Dates were a major source of sweetness for the ancient Hebrews who, like the Bedouins of today, had a use for every part of the stately palm tree.*

below: *Wheat has kept its importance for mankind throughout the ages: nothing yet has replaced the savour of a fresh wheaten loaf.*

below right: *Barley has declined in importance, especially since the horse and the ox, its major customers for fodder, gave way to the machine.*

right: *Figs, growing wild or cultivated, eaten fresh or dried, were familiar to all in the days of the Bible.*

The grape, eaten fresh or yielding wine or raisins, is valued, in legend and in truth, by the fox and the jackal and by man.

Less easy to eat than the apple or the pear, these cannot compare with the pomegranate for beauty, colour, taste and fragrance.

right: Only a few days old, the fawn of the gazelle already raises its head with all the characteristic elegance and grace of its species.

PLANT AND WILD LIFE IN THE BIBLE

The Land of the Bible has the distinction of being a place familiar to millions of people who have never visited it and who can never hope to do so. There must be many in distant lands who had heard of Jerusalem and Jericho before they even knew the name of the capital city in the country of their birth, and this all because of one book, that book of books which has had a greater influence on mankind than any other, the Bible.

The Bible was not only written in Israel; it grew out of it. The religious and social philosophy it contains could perhaps have been born elsewhere, but the way in which these thoughts are expressed and the imagery used bear the indelible imprint of her countryside.

What is left to us of the world of the Bible? Where are the hills and the valleys, the plants and the animals which it describes? Does anything still remain of the environment which did so much to lend immediacy to its prophecies, meaning to its laws and imagery to its poetry?

An archaeologist would be amused by such questions. There is hardly a place or a material object mentioned in the Bible which he cannot produce for inspection — and we do not mean a reconstruction, but the real thing. What place would you fancy? Beth Shean or Megiddo perhaps, or Jaffa, whence Jonah embarked for Nineveh, or the well of Harod from which Gideon's men drank? Or perhaps you would like a clay pitcher, penates (ancient household gods), letters from ancient Lachish or scrolls from Qumran? They are all to be found here. In the dry air of the

Judean desert a mat of rushes was recently found in a state of perfect preservation after 6,000 years, and it can be seen today in the Israel Museum in Jerusalem. And what about the oak and the terebinth, the gazelle and the vulture? Are they legendary or can they be seen today, just as they were then, and thus reveal some new insight into the Bible?

Obviously much has changed, both for better and for worse, in the past thousands of years. If one of the Jews of ancient times were to rise from his grave today and come to Israel he might at first be startled by the changes in the landscape, some brought about by the destructions of earlier generations and some arising from the constructions of later ones. Even so, after he had grown accustomed to these super-ficial changes, he might well arrive at the conclusion that it is still the country that he knew. Not only have the timeless hills and valleys remained as they were, but the vegetation which clothes them is the same, and the animals that wander at large.

Broad observations about the landscape of the countryside, its plant and wild life, can have little value and it might be better, rather, to take as our starting point the more extreme contrasts which we may encounter within the confines of this relatively small area. In a later chapter we will go into more detail, and even attempt to explain these contrasts in the light of present knowledge. For the moment we will just mention that, growing alongside plants that are especially well adapted to conditions of absolute dryness (xerophytes) or extreme saltiness (halophytes), we may find mesophytes, plants that require abundant moisture, damp soil and fresh water; that we may find amphibians which cannot survive long away from water living in close proximity to creatures so well adjusted to desert conditions that they produce very concentrated urine, or urea crystals, so that not a single drop of moisture shall be wasted; and that in the heart of arid desert you may come upon an oasis of fresh running water surrounded by water plants.

The struggle between the desert and the forest and, at a later period, between desert and settled areas, is reflected in writings from the very earliest recorded time. The expatriate Egyptian Sinuhe, who lived in the 20th century BC, wrote enthusiastically about the country: '. . . and there were figs and vines, and its wine was more plentiful than water. Its honey was in abundance and its oil magnificent. Every fruit grew on its trees and its barley and wheat were beyond measure.' A hundred years later, an Egyptian artist painted a caravan of Canaanites bringing the produce of their land to Egypt, the perfumes, asses and gazelles symbolizing the union of desert and settlement. Six hundred years later, Moses sent his men from the wilderness of Paran to spy out the land of Canaan. They brought back a cluster of grapes that they had to bear 'between two upon a staff; and they brought of the pomegranates, and of the figs.' (Numbers 13: 23).

Botanists do not agree as to whether the common oak is by nature a shrub or a tree. These ancient oaks, near a sacred tomb in Galilee, stand silent and provide an answer.

Rocks in a vineyard can be troublesome and must be removed, but can be used to make a useful watchtower, reminding us of the one referred to by the Prophet Isaiah.

The two things which make the deepest impression on the traveller on his first visit to Israel, and which appear to him so typical of the country, are the prickly pear (*Opuntia ficus-indica*) and the camel. The native born Jews are even called *sabras*, the local name for prickly pear, because, according to one school of thought they are prickly on the surface and sweet inside. Curiously enough, both prickly pears, and camels, are relative newcomers to the land. The prickly pear was introduced from America, via North Africa, within the past 200 years, and it did not even have any close relatives here. The camel (*Camelus dromedarius*) is of somewhat less recent origin; it is believed to have been brought here by the Midianites during the time of Gideon, 3,200 years ago.

Where, then, are the truly native sons? A good number are invisible to all but the naturalist. They are just too small to be seen easily. The Bible summed them up in

Stone Age scythes were made of jaw bones with flint blades. Flint and bone have been replaced by iron, but the method of reaping has not changed.

a phrase: 'A land of wheat, and barley, and vines, and fig trees, and pomegranates; a land of oil olive, and honey.' (Deuteronomy 8:8). Jewish folklore calls them the 'seven species' and they are regarded as the symbol of the country's fertility. Barley may be less important since the internal combustion engine replaced the horse, and some of the fruits mentioned may not be able to vie with apples and pears, but the picture conjured up by the 'seven species' is still valid.

The types of wheat and barley cultivated in Israel today may bear foreign names, and several of them were imported from distant lands, but stalks of the aboriginal wild varieties still wave on the hills of Galilee and Judea and they are the ancestors of wheat and barley the world over. Farmers and geneticists looking for a remedy for the diseases and pests which affect the more delicate modern varieties seek to breed from the wild plants, which have become resistant to many diseases.

The olive, the fig and the date, which is sometimes referred to in the Bible as honey because of the sweet syrup which was made from them, have some claim to have originated in Israel. While there is no real proof that these trees derive from native wild varieties there is no evidence to the contrary. Their forebears are believed to have appeared first in the region of North Africa, Asia Minor and the Arabian desert, and we still find their wild relatives growing in Israel.

The date (*Phoenix dactylifera*) is the 'staff of life' of the desert. According to the Arabic saying, 'its head should be in fire and its feet in water.' In other words, it needs a lot of sun — otherwise the fruit cannot ripen — and water. Dates do not grow in dry soil, and are a sure sign that there is water below ground at that spot. In the deserts of the Negev and Sinai, the date palms rising up out of the sands, the sweet fruits dangling from their crowns, draw both man and beast. The Bedouin of today, like the Hebrews of old, has a use for every part of the date palm; not only the fruit, but also the trunk and leaves are used. It is sometimes difficult to decide whether the palm we see is really wild or whether it may not have sprung from a date stone cast there by some Bedouin a generation or so ago. In the past Israel was a date-growing centre, but neglect reduced the industry to one of minor importance. In recent years date cultivation has been taken up again by modern Jewish farmers.

Throughout the centuries the olive (*Olea europaea*) has been regarded as the source of the country's wealth. It could be said of any hill village, almost without exception, that its economy is based on the olive and the black and green fruit from its olive groves. The success the Jews enjoyed in cultivating olives was one of the attractions that drew the Romans to this country. The modern Arabic proverb has it that 'gardens (including both vegetables and orchards) are folly, and olives are kings.' The trees themselves, which live to scores and even hundreds of years, express their character as well as their age in their thick, gnarled trunks. They are the true symbol of the country.

The Arabs grew a variety of olive which bears small fruit with a large stone and meagre flesh, but yielding much oil. The modern Jewish farmers have introduced other varieties, whose fruit is better suited for table use though less rich in oil. Wild olives, possibly the forebears of the groves of today, may still be found on the Carmel range and in the hills of Galilee.

The fig (*Ficus carica*) never enjoyed the high esteem that was accorded to the date and the olive, simply because it was never so vital to life or to the economy, but its fruit played an important role in the diet of the inhabitants of the country. Whether eaten fresh during the two months that the trees are fruit-bearing, or dried during the rest of the year, figs provided an important source of nourishment and sweetness. In the parable told by Jothem in the Book of Judges, the fig tree was mentioned in the same breath as the vine and the olive as a productive tree which had no time for

'That ancient river, the river Kishon…',
a trickle in summer, but swollen here
by the winter rains.

foolishness (Judges 9: 8–15). It can be found both cultivated and wild, while related species also grow wild here.

Both the vine (*Vitis vinifera*) and the pomegranate, unlike the others of the 'seven species' mentioned above, are the sole representatives of their families in Israel, and nobody can point to any related tree which would testify to their origin here. Nevertheless, their development can be traced back to the very beginning of agricultural cultivation. Green or black, eaten fresh, or as raisins or wine, or made into jam, the country would not be the same without them. Sometimes you can see a vine rich in years climbing up the side of a house to the second storey, with its leaves and shoots spreading out from a thick trunk to cover an entire balcony, and studded here and there with thick bunches of grapes.

The pomegranate (*Punica granatum*) is the most decorative of the 'seven species' but the least essential and the most difficult to eat. With its perfectly rounded shape, its rich colour ranging from every shade of green to red, and its little coronet, there is no fruit quite like it. Within, the abundance of juicy red seeds draws the eye and whets the appetite. Its origin was certainly in Israel or the surrounding area, though no one can be sure exactly where.

Other native plants, and some of the animals which inhabit the land, will be described in later chapters, laying stress upon their connection with the biblical texts. Although the ordinary reader regards the Bible mainly as a religious text or a book of morals, or simply as literature, he may still be interested in the surroundings from which these ideas came. In the following chapters we shall try to throw light upon the natural phenomena of the Land of the Bible, and hope to give the reader a more vivid perception of some of the passages whose imagery springs from this natural setting.

'...from the cedar tree that is in Lebanon even to the hyssop that springeth out of the wall.'

(I Kings 4:33)

The juniper, whose home is in the Lebanon, is a rare tree in Israel, to be found only in one small group on a high mountain in Upper Galilee.

AT THE CROSS ROADS OF THREE CONTINENTS

A few decades ago, naturalists who tried to draw up a map of the plant life of the Land of Israel found themselves faced with an abundant and confusing assortment of plants of different origins and types. It was relatively simple to map the hill country in the north, where the vegetation was typically Mediterranean, very much like that to be found in Greece or Italy. The few scientists who ventured south to the Judean desert and the lower Negev found it equally easy to report the predominance of typically desert vegetation. But it was much more difficult to bring some sort of logical order into the results of field studies in the area between the north and the south, where it seemed impossible to establish the boundary between one zone of vegetation and another.

It was easy to see that Israel is undoubtedly a crossroads for different types of plant and animal life, but the question remained as to where to locate the actual meeting place, and to explain how it came about. A brilliant naturalist, Alexander Eig, produced an original and simple answer in the summary of a botanical study he made of the country during the 1920's. Today, we are used to the maps which he drew up himself or which were made by those who followed in his footsteps, and the whole situation seems very clear, but then it was a major discovery.

From a map of the region we see that, geographically, Israel lies at the crossroads of Eurasia and Africa, and close to the border of Asia and Europe. It is therefore located at the meeting place of three continents, and the connecting link from Eurasia to Africa through Israel and Sinai follows a narrow strip of land. These

Low scattered shrubs throughout the year, with grasses and flowers in winter; this is the landscape of the steppe in the northern Negev. Only in the beds of streams and similar depressions can a richer vegetation develop.

are simple facts; but what implications can they have for the plant and animal kingdoms?

If this geographical contact had been established along a region of the latitude, say, of the British Isles, or if the Mediterranean had receded so that it would not influence the schematic outline of climatic regions, everything would have been different. Moving northwards, the transition would have been from desert to steppe, succeeded in turn by woodland. Even though the sequence to the east of the land of Israel is as we have described — desert, steppe, woodland — on the west, the Mediterranean zone reaches right up to the edge of the desert, producing the special landscape of Israel.

The basic problem of creating order in the chaos of plant distribution was solved when Eig realized that this country is not only a meeting place between woodland and desert, but that the steppes to the east also enter into the equation, and even the

A grasshopper, perfectly adapted to the life of the desert. Though its dark colouring shows up against its surroundings, its poisonous secretions ensure that it will not be devoured by prospective enemies.

Date palms grow right down to the sea on the coast of Sinai. They also thrive in the sands of the central desert, finding ways to reach water even there. Perhaps the Children of Israel halted at this spot, in their wanderings after they left Egypt.

right: *A wall built by King Uzziah more than 2,500 years ago. In the course of time it has become an integral part of the landscape, natural habitat of desert reptiles and insects.*

Slim and elegant, the Sinai agama is strictly a desert dweller, keeping to places where rocks abound.

distant tropics. Let us now look at the characteristics of each region. The decisive factor is climate, especially fluctuations in temperature, and quantity and distribution of rainfall. As far as these elements are concerned, there are sharp differences between one part of Israel and another, and it would be best first to examine each zone separately.

1. MEDITERRANEAN ZONE. Its most outstanding climatic feature is its dry, not too hot, summer. Rainfall of twenty to forty inches a year is concentrated into the winter months, when temperatures only rarely drop below freezing. The rainy season really begins in October, though there are generally a few scattered showers in September, reaching a climax in December and January, and continuing into April. Between the end of one rainy season and the beginning of the next, showers are rare. On the other hand, the precipitation value of the summer dews can amount to ten inches a year.

Such conditions can support natural woodlands, generally evergreen and maquis. And just such woodland can be found extending over thousands of acres, though this certainly represents only a faint shadow of what once was there. Vestiges which have remained in various places, as well as the historical accounts which have survived, leave no doubt that before man appeared and cleared away most of the forests to make way for his farms, woodlands covered most of the Mediterranean zone. Depending on the type of soil, amount of rainfall and range of temperature, various types of forest growth developed. Four principal types resemble those which we find in other Mediterranean lands. They consist of Jerusalem pine forest (*Pinus halepensis*); deciduous forests of Mount Tabor oaks (*Quercus ithaburensis*) growing together with styrax (*Styrax officionalis*), terebinth and others; carob (*Ceratonias siliqua*) and lentisc or mastich tree (*Pistacia lentiscus*) forests; and lastly the maquis of common oak (*Quercus calliprinos*) and Palestine terebinth (*Pistacia palaestina*) of which we will have more to say later. In only a few places does the Mediterranean zone terminate abruptly. Generally, the transition from Mediterranean to a neighbouring zone is a very gradual one.

Looking like a typical spring in Galilee, strangely enough it is in the Judean Desert, at Ein Gedi. Everywhere within reach of the water are reeds, tamarisks and even fig trees. A step beyond, the desert holds sway.

The maidenhair fern is found all over the world, and is not uncommon in Israel wherever there is shade and water.

2. THE IRANO-TURANIAN STEPPE. The great steppes of central and south-west Asia are represented only in miniature in Israel, even by the modest standards of the country. A narrow strip of steppe surrounds the Mediterranean zone, separating it from and connecting it to the desert areas.

In contrast to some of the great steppes of Asia, the element which distinguishes the Israeli version is not the cold but the dryness. Annual rainfall never exceeds ten inches, with effective rainfall confined to the four winter months between December and March. Eight months of the year are almost totally dry, and this factor is what chiefly determines the character of the plant life. What kind of vegetation can survive under such conditions? Annuals for which the short rainy season meets the needs of their entire life cycle, from budding to seeding; plants which can survive the dry season in some kind of dormant state, e.g. bulbous plants (geophytes), or bushes which shed their leaves in the summer; trees or brush which have evolved some kind of mechanism for surviving extreme arid conditions; and lastly, plants which take advantage of special terrain, such as wadi beds and other declivities, where some water is generally retained.

The steppe area looks quite different from the Mediterranean zone or the adjacent desert. In winter and spring it is covered with green, blanketed with flowering annuals and blossoming bushes. In the parts which enjoy slightly more rain, the vegetation covers the area almost completely. As summer draws near only the bushes remain, part green and part greyish. In the desert, there is no plant life whatsoever to be seen in the summer.

As we have already noted, the steppe area forms a belt all round the Mediterranean zone, constituting a buffer between it and the desert. In most places this belt is quite narrow; along the slope that faces the Jordan River, for example, the transition from Mediterranean zone to desert is a mile or two at most. This, by the

The oasis of Ein Gedi is a meeting place for plant and animal species from far and wide. The moringa tree from the Sudan bears pink blossom in the spring and develops long seed pods.

30

Water — essential ingredient in the magic of the oasis. The swiftly flowing Wadi Qelt sustains a lush vegetation, but one step beyond the water's reach the desert holds sway.

Stones in the far south: these strange formations, like well-baked loaves, catch the eye in the arid desert near Eilat.

left: *The vegetation of the Asian steppe is here represented by dwarf grasses and shrubs, connecting and dividing the Mediterranean and Desert zones.*

The cony, a typical African species, thrives on the rocky mountains all over Israel.

The tropical doum palms (Hyphaene thebaica), of Africa, growing here in the Arava valley north of Eilat.

below: Alpine vegetation in the far north: rounded bushes of acantholimon on Mount Hermon.

way, was one of the chief factors that confused the early botanists. Only in the Beersheba plain does the steppe widen out into a broad area, up to the Hebron hills in the north. To the south, it stretches a finger out into the desert and the Negev uplands. East of the Jordan the steppe broadens again, merging gradually into the Arabian desert.

3. THE DESERT ZONE. Later on we shall devote an entire chapter to the desert, which it surely deserves, but it must be mentioned here too, as part of the over-all picture of plant and animal life. The Saharo-Arabian Desert, as its name implies, runs from the coast of north-west Africa, through the Sahara, Libya and Egypt and on to the Arabian peninsula. It is hot and arid, with negligible rainfall (up to four inches per year) — and even this figure does not give a true picture of what the desert is like. There are times when the entire rainfall pours down in one torrential deluge, washing away everything in its path and literally changing the very face of the country, and this may be followed by two practically rainless years. Under such conditions, plant life can only survive by evolving some very special features, and then only in certain parts of the desert.

In Israel the desert is bounded on the west by Sinai, includes most of the Negev, and penetrates northwards deep into the Jordan Valley. To the south, it encircles the Mediterranean and steppe areas in the high hills of Edom and links up with the expanses of the Arabian desert.

An interesting phenomenon is the penetration of the desert northwards along the sands of the Mediterranean beaches. There, all along the shore, a scene of desert vegetation opens out, mingling with the plants of the Mediterranean zone. The operative factor is not the low rainfall, but the fact that all the moisture is swallowed up by the sands, so that here a desert landscape coincides with quite generous precipitation.

There are few water holes in the desert, and springs are even more rare, but when the combination of water and heat does occur it produces a new scene entirely — the desert oasis. And this brings us to the fourth zone.

4. THE SUDANESE ZONE. While the three zones described so far represent unbroken extensions of their parent areas, we now come to one which is completely detached. Oases are islands of vegetation which are often hundreds and perhaps even thousands of miles away from their normal habitat. An interesting question in itself is just how the distinctive plant life managed to get there, across the barren desert. One theory holds that such growths are the vestiges of an unbroken African tropical jungle which flourished during some distant past, where today there is only desert. When the rains failed, it is suggested, the vegetation withered away from the arid areas, leaving only these tiny enclaves centred around sources of water. In terms of total area this zone comprises only a small proportion of the country;

Water, still or running, attracts a flora of its own, one of whose features is its ubiquity. Two sedges shown here (right) *are amongst eighteen species of the genus to be found throughout the greater part of the northern hemisphere and, as with sorrel* (left), *usually near water.*

all the oases together, even including the Jordan Valley, amount to less than one per cent of the total area of the land of Israel. But then, size is not everything; of the sixty species of trees growing wild in Israel, ten or a dozen are indigenous to the oases of the Sudanese zone.

Here it is worth mentioning another tropical 'invasion' (as a matter of fact, this is not an invasion, but rather the rear guard of the tropical vegetation which once covered the country): two species of tree, the *Acacia albida* and the Christ-thorn (*Zizyphus spina-christi*). These two native tropical plants are not uncommon, the acacia growing in small clumps in river beds and the thorn either in groups or even alone in almost every part of the country. Many of the Christ-thorn trees are hundreds of years old and of considerable size. Some of them owe their longevity to the reverence in which they were held.

The division of the country into four zones of plant life suggests the origin of the vegetation. Yet plants native to opposite ends of the earth can be found growing side by side. Apart from the main groupings there are also representatives of such exotic and distant climes as Siberia, North America and South Africa. The plants which are indigenous to these places must surely have a story to tell of how they came to be here.

From what we have said so far it is easy to understand why the number of plant species to be found in Israel is so far out of proportion to its area. In all, 2,500 species of flowering plants have been classified, and new discoveries — some of them altogether new to science — are found every year.

For many of the species, Israel represents the limit of their distribution. This is the eastern limit for many Mediterranean varieties, the western boundary of some steppeland species, the northern extent of African plant life and the southern limit of the few Euro-Siberian plants to be found. It is not surprising therefore that, in a

small country where the variations of climate can accommodate such a wide variety of species, it is possible to find such a wide range of types concentrated in a small area. One such place was the Lake Hula region — today a nature reserve, where the lake used to be. Here, to mention only members of the international family of reeds, grow such dissimilar varieties as the tropical papyrus (*Cyperus papyrus*), the European frog's bit (*Hydrocharis morsus-ranae*) and assorted Mediterranean reeds.

Sometimes the transition from the plant life typical of one region to that of another extends over a broad area, where the two kinds are intermingled, in places, in what at first glance appears to be an unlikely mixture. For example, there are east-west ravines where the southern wall, which faces north and is therefore cooler, will be covered with Mediterranean foliage, while the northern one, which is generally hotter and drier, supports only steppeland growths, whereas on the level land between the two walls the plant life of the regions intermingles.

Especially striking are those places where, because of some geographical or topographical peculiarity, the transition is sudden. Along the mountain ridge from Jerusalem southward, Mediterranean-type plant life can support itself only up to the verge of the land falling away to the east. From this point eastwards the amount of rainfall decreases drastically and the Mediterranean vegetation quickly gives place to that typical of the steppe, and just as suddenly this vanishes into classically desert territory.

Another site where the transition is particularly sharp is the Makhtesh Ramon, in the central Negev. A plateau rises beyond the northern wall of the crater to a height of more than 3,000 feet above sea level. There is enough rainfall here to support steppe vegetation, and in springtime most of it turns green and comes into flower. The wall of the Makhtesh itself is an almost sheer precipice, descending 1,200 feet to the floor of the crater, a flat, sandy desert terrain in sharp contrast to the steppe-land plant life up above.

37

The maquis of western Galilee, with the Crusader castle of Montfort on the skyline. The plantain in the foreground illustrates the northern features of the vegetation in this area.

*Bracken, common in Europe but rare in Israel,
is to be found in the heart of tall forests.*

The Hula nature reserve is another meeting place for plants: here the frog's-bit from Siberia grows at the feet of the tropical papyrus.

And then there are the desert oases; the presence of water here is enough to support fresh green vegetation even during the hottest days of summer. Yet venture as much as an inch beyond the water's range and the greenery stops short, as if cut away by a knife, and the desert takes over again. There can be no sharper contrast than between the lush water plants and Sudanese vegetation of the oasis and the dry, Saharo-Arabian desert growths that surround them.

Among the plants of the Sudanese region in Israel, the doum palm (*Hyphaene thebaica*), which grows near Eilat, is worth mentioning. Its wide fronds grow from a multiple trunk, which is very unusual in palm trees. In all, there are only three clumps of these palms in the whole of Israel — more than a thousand miles from their nearest relatives in East Africa.

Amongst the plant life here are some species whose origins can be traced back to the dim past, and others of relatively recent settlement — only a few million years. These latter still retain some trace of their foreign antecedents, and sometimes flower at seasons which are hardly appropriate to the general rhythm of life in Israel. The acacia and the carob, for instance, come into blossom at the end of the summer; this may be the best time in the climate of their native Africa, but it is not the normal habit here. A comparatively new arrival, the evening primrose (*Oenothera*), was introduced from America only two centuries ago and has made itself completely at home in the sands along the seashore, while other 'invaders' from distant lands have turned into wild plants, and even degenerated into noxious weeds in their new environment.

There are 150 species of plants endemic to Israel and found nowhere else in the world. Good examples of these are most of the large species of iris. With their very special ecological requirements, they thrive in the transitional type of conditions between Mediterranean region and steppe.

Pond-weed, the seeds of which were probably carried here on the feet of water birds.

The wide range of climatic conditions in Israel favours the growth of an equally wide variety of plants from distant regions. More than 1,000 varieties of fruit-bearing and decorative plants are cultivated, and the list grows longer with each passing year. A visitor from a far-off land should not be surprised to find some species, which he thought to be characteristic of his own country, growing as if they belonged here. Even some of the fruits which are regarded as almost exclusively Israeli are really interlopers which immigrated only recently. Our oranges, known and sought after throughout the world as 'Jaffas', came from China no earlier than the 16th century. Brought to this country by Portuguese traders, the name for them in Arabic to this day is *bordegan*, a corruption of the word Portugal.

Israel is a regional crossroads in the animal kingdom as well, and can boast representatives from all the regions mentioned earlier, in connection with their plant life. Obviously, it is not quite as simple to pinpoint specific areas as being the habitat of certain animals as it is for plant life. For example, a half-mile strip of steppe dividing the Mediterranean region from the reaches of the eastern desert has practically no significance as far as animal life is concerned. Nevertheless, a zoologist blocking out the areas of habitation of various species of animal on a map of the world would come to much the same conclusion as the botanist: that Israel is a meeting place of widely differing regions.

The waters of the Mediterranean are linked, even though narrowly, with the Atlantic. But, divided from these seas only by the Sinai Peninsula, the Gulf of Aqaba and the Red Sea are extensions of the Indian Ocean, and a list of the marine life of the Mediterranean would have little relevance for someone studying the sea off Eilat. There he would be beginning again, with something completely different.

For wolves (*Canis lupus*), Israel is the southernmost extremity of their range, and it may be observed that the further south they appear, the smaller they become,

A fig tree growing out of an ancient wall in Galilee: self-sown, it bears poor fruit.

until they finally fade from the scene. The wolves that roam the northern part of the country closely resemble those of Europe, though smaller in size, while in the Negev there are several packs of small wolves, hardly larger than jackals. There are no wolves at all on the continent of Africa.

The cony (*Procavia capensis*), on the other hand, is at the northernmost limit of its habitation in Israel and Syria. Indigenous to Africa, they roam throughout that continent, from the Cape to the Levant. In Israel they dwell in the hills, in all types of climate, from the desert around Eilat to the forests of Galilee.

The role of meeting place, however, is probably most readily seen in bird migration. The migratory phenomenon is familiar, of course, wherever birds appear or disappear with the change of seasons. In Israel, though, we are literally at the crossroads of their lines of flight. European and African birds generally follow the great rift along the Arava and the Jordan Valley or else the Mediterranean coastline, where their lines of flight take them over Israel during their migrations. For some birds this is the southernmost limit of their travels, while for others this is the farthest north they ever come. Here they mingle with the permanent residents, as well as with visitors from distant climes. The palm dove (*Streptopelia senegalensis*), which settled here from its native Senegal in West Africa only recently, has made itself as much at home in Israeli towns as its indigenous Israeli relative, the village-dwelling collared turtle dove (*S. decaoto*), and the plain turtle dove (*S. turtur*), of whose summer visits Jeremiah said, '. . . and the turtle and the crane and the swallow observe the time of their coming.'

'While the earth remaineth, seedtime and harvest, and cold and heat, and summer and winter, and day and night shall not cease.'

(Genesis 8:22)

The sunflower does full justice to its name; turning to face the sun all day, it also looks like one.

THE YEAR HAS TWO SEASONS

The concept of four seasons of the year is deeply entrenched and long current in literature, in art and in every aspect of life, and when it is suggested that, as a matter of fact, there are only two seasons in Israel it is only natural that all sorts of objections should be raised. The Bible is cited as the authority and the passages which specifically mention summer and winter, spring and autumn, are brought as proof of their existence. In support of our contention we must therefore show which two seasons are missing.

It may come as a surprise to some people to learn that there is no mention of four seasons in the Bible. The Hebrew word *stav*, translated today as autumn, appears only once in the Scriptures, in that wonderful passage in the Song of Solomon (2: 11) where it is rendered in the Authorized Version as, 'For lo, the winter is past, the rain is over and gone . . .' *Stav*, according to most scholars, is winter, or the time of the winter rains. The Hebrew word *aviv*, which today is used to mean spring, appears twice in the Bible, to denote not a season, but a stage in the ripening of barley. *Hodesh ha'aviv*, translated as 'the month of Abib' in the Authorized Version, is the month when this particular ripening process takes place — the Hebrew month of Nissan. There is no mention in the Bible of a season called spring. Nor is the word *aviv*, which appears in all seven times, ever rendered as spring in the English version. So in fact the Bible recognizes only two seasons, summer and winter or, as they were known to the authors of the Talmud, 'the days of sun' and 'the days of rain.' Under the influence of Greco-Roman civilization, the Jews of

The blue squill is only one of many harbingers of spring, but one of the most conspicuous.

*The turtle dove is a summer
visitor in Israel, arriving from
Africa when the other birds have
already begun nesting.*

Talmudic times divided the year into four seasons, though always by using the original Hebrew names of the months in which each season began. They were the time of Tishri (October), the time of Tevet (January), the time of Nissan (April) and the time of Tammuz (July). This is how they are also identified in the rare mosaic worked into the floor of the sixth century synagogue which was found at Beth Alfa.

Now that we have scriptural backing for our assertion that the year in Israel is divided into two seasons only, we can go on to describe the actual climate of the country and the way these seasons present themselves.

Israel is situated in an area of winter rains, and it is only natural that the first climatic characteristic we shall consider is rainfall. Rain, or the lack of it, more than any other single factor, determines the character of the different regions in every aspect from the contours of the landscape to the type of cultivation, or absence of it, and even the distribution of its population. If the year divides naturally into two basic seasons, the rainy season and the hot season, the period during which they overlap varies considerably from place to place and from year to year.

Israel is a country of sharp contrasts. A question as to what kind of weather is to be expected there in any particular month would be completely meaning-less without specifying the locality. In Safed for instance, north of the Sea of

Winter, depicted in a charmingly primitive way, in a section of the mosaic floor of the ancient synagogue of Beth Alfa (sixth century AD), where it is called 'Season of Tevet' (January).

Sunflowers, like other summer blooms in unirrigated land, whether wild or cultivated, are especially well adapted for extracting moisture from the dry earth.

The magic of spring is manifest in every land.
Here it brings a 'living carpet' of flowers to the
slope of a small hill in the northern Negev, where
the desert normally holds sway.

*As the autumn sun sets, the dry thistle heads and
the gathering clouds are a reminder that the rainy
season is not far off.*

Oranges, the main crop of modern Israel, adorn the landscape in the rainy season with their brightly coloured juicy fruits.

Galilee, it is wise to take a coat when going on an outing in August, while in Eilat a bathe in the sea in January is enjoyable. Yet if, after basking there in the sun for a few hours, you make the fifty-minute air trip to Lod (Lydda), you may well run into rain and biting cold winds. Thus a statement that the hot season extends from May to October, and the rainy season from November until the end of April, would have to be qualified by an indication of the locality referred to. Generally, the rainy season becomes longer the farther north one goes. If the term winter is taken to mean the colder time of the year, then the Negev desert has its winter too, though it would be nonsense to speak of a rainy season there. In the area of Eilat the entire annual rainfall — averaging about one inch — may fall in one torrential downpour in September or May, while the whole of the winter will be without rain.

In the Mediterranean zone there are real rains, with anything from seventeen to forty inches a year considered normal. This is enough to support field crops, vineyards and unirrigated orchards, and in uncultivated areas forest vegetation grows well. As a rule the rains begin at the end of October, though a September downpour is not unusual. Even in these days of widespread irrigation farmers look wistfully to the sky for signs of rain, and it is not hard to imagine what it was like in times past, as this little story from the Talmud shows: An unbeliever came to Rabbi Yehoshua ben Carha and said, 'We have our holidays and you have your holidays. When are our hearts gladdened together?' to which Rabbi Yehoshua replied, 'When it rains.'

There was always a special significance attached to the first rain. A modern plough can break up the driest soil, but the implements which were available to the ancient Hebrews — like those still used by the *fellahin* (peasants) — could only make a furrow in damp earth. Because of its significance the first rain has a special name of its own, the *yoreh* — the first 'shot'.

From October onwards, between four and eight inches fall every month, depending on the locality and the year. During a drought year the amount may be as little as half the average. For areas at the edges of the Mediterranean zone this can spell disaster. But the amount of rain alone is not the decisive factor; its distribution during the season is of overriding importance. A cloudburst that precipitates four inches of rain onto parched earth in a brief downpour is less useful than half this amount falling evenly over a month.

Just as the first rain determines the farmer's prospects for the year so, by the time the last rain, the *malkosh*, falls at the end of March or in early April, he knows whether his hopes of the winter have been realized. 'They that sow in tears shall reap in joy' (Psalms 126: 5) is a verse that is rooted in the agricultural realities of Israel, like the much later Talmudic discussions that went something like this: In the Biblical injunctions dealing with the festivals it is said of *Succot* (Feast of

Little more than a generation ago, the fields, orange groves and fishponds around Ein Harod, seen here from Mount Gilboa, were malaria-infested swamps.

right: *A deciduous oak in winter: its branches were lopped by* fellahin *(Arab peasants) in an attempt to obtain a long straight growth of timber for building.*

Tabernacles) in October 'Rejoice in your festival' three times, while rejoicing is not mentioned even once in connection with *Pesach* (Passover), which coincides with Eastertide. Why? Because at Passover the fate of the grain is still being decided and no one yet knows whether it will be a good harvest or not, whereas by the time of *Succot* both grain and fruit crops have already been harvested.

The further north or the higher into the mountains we go, the colder and wetter the winters become. As a rule, winter temperatures do not fall below freezing in the daylight hours, though night frosts are not uncommon and in the mountains even snow is no rarity. On very rare occasions snow covers the entire country — 1950 was one of those years, and the previous one was in 1807. On the other hand, in cities at a high altitude, like Safed and Jerusalem, snow is not so rare and a real blizzard occurs once in every decade or so. On Mount Hermon drifts of snow linger on throughout most of the summer. The climate of the mountains of Transjordan resembles that on the west bank of the river.

left: *One of many bulbous plants in Israel, the fritillaria is unique with its bell-like greenish flowers.*

Spring in Israel is the season of abundant orange blossom, filling the landscape with rich creamy flowers and the air with heady perfume.

The rainfall decreases sharply as we move southwards or eastwards from the Mediterranean zone. Of special interest is the rapid decline in rainfall figures moving eastwards from the mountain ridge of Judea and Samaria, down the slopes which are said to be 'in the shadow of the rain.' The annual average is twenty-eight inches in the Hebron and Judean hills, but declines rapidly with each succeeding mile eastward. Five miles beyond Hebron we find ourselves in desert country.

The area in which the annual average rainfall is about six to eight inches is defined as *arava*, or steppe. Here, the precipitation is not enough to sustain woodland but can give bare support to brush, with an occasional tree where there is some hidden source of water to be tapped; the hot season becomes longer at the expense of the rainy season and, with few exceptions, trees cannot survive the interval. Orchards require irrigation and even field crops fail occasionally. Drought is an all too frequent visitor.

From here it is only a short step to the desert, where the annual average rainfall is less than six inches. As we mentioned earlier, the term rainy season can only be used in its calendar sense. In the desert the entire growing season is condensed into the months from January to March, and the dry season takes over for the rest of the year. This does not mean, of course, that nights out in the hot desert are not bitterly cold in winter — colder by far than in the Mediterranean zone.

The rains in the northern part of the land are generally absorbed into the soil, and only rarely cause floods. In former years, when there were still swamps, the rains

could lead to flooding, but since the land has been drained this problem no longer arises. One may recall here the famous war between the Israelites, under the Judges, Barak and Deborah, and the Canaanites under Sisera, in ancient times. The Bible tells how the 'Stars in their courses fought against Sisera', but another passage enlightens us further by explaining how this heavenly intervention manifested itself: 'The river of Kishon swept them away.' Anyone who is acquainted with winter in the Jezreel Valley can well imagine the actual course of events. The battle took place on a winter's day; a sudden rainstorm caught the Canaanite host in their war chariots, in the middle of the valley, and they were stuck in the mud. The lightly armed warriors of the Israelites, who generally found themselves in unequal combat against these chariots, were able to take the advantage of the Canaanites in their muddy plight, the Canaanites lost their army, and the Israelites saw the hand of Heaven in their victory. In the Negev the rains have a different effect, as will be explained in a later chapter.

If the winter had a clearly defined ending we could look forward to the spring, but things do not turn out quite like that. Beautiful spring days in the European sense occur here and there during the drizzly winter, from January on. Then the grass turns green, the flowers bloom, and when out walking you may suddenly have to take off your jacket and roll up your sleeves. Such lovely days can be followed by heavy rain and bitter cold, and then the cycle repeats itself again.

Dark velvety sheathes, each with a spike at its centre, and growing straight from the ground with the first rain, they do not look like flowers. But they are; more precisely, the inflorescence of the biarum.

Neither March, April nor May can be said to be the end of the rain and cold, heralding a gradual change to warmer weather. Rather the winter, with the spring days it also has to offer, is cut off sharply by the onset of a week of scorching heat: *sharav* in Hebrew. The mercury, which had fluctuated between 60°F (16°C) in the hills and 80°F (27°C) in the south, suddenly surges up to 90°F (32°C) and 110°F (43°C) respectively. The characteristics of the *sharav* are an oppressively hot, dry east wind coupled with a dusty haze in the air. Within a week, the entire landscape changes from green to sere yellow. Yet the *sharav*, too, can be followed by thunderstorms and rain, and days of cold and damp return. This cycle can be repeated several times, with or without rain, during April and May. It is not only the newcomers to Israel who suffer in these periods of heatwave; no one seems able to get used to them.

*Showing young and delicate leaves at
the beginning of winter, in their full
growth at winter's end these plants
will become tall and spiteful thistles*

Perhaps it is these few days of extreme heat that cause people to think of Israel as a
very hot country, though in fact it is not so.

In the desert the hot season begins in March but in Galilee not until April or May,
and the transition from wet to hot season, or from winter to summer, can come
very suddenly. While there is no clearly defined and regular season which can be
called spring, it would be wrong to say that the phenomenon of spring does not exist.
Life renews itself in winter. The 15th of the Hebrew month of Shvat, which generally
falls in February, is celebrated as the beginning of the budding season, and its
emblem is the flowering almond tree. In the months between this festival and the
middle of May, the countryside is in full bloom. Wild grasses and thistles thrust
up out of the soil to become man-high plants, and deciduous forest and fruit trees
begin to bud and blossom. Yet during this same brief spring another part of the
vegetation turns yellow and withers away at the very moment when the rest is
entering upon the first stages of its life cycle.

A careful look at the animal kingdom shows that, here too, the greatest changes
take place at this season. Bird migration is on the move and, what may be of greater
interest, bird nesting. Some of the smallest, and also some of the very large birds,
begin to build their nests as early as February, though the majority come into full
activity in April, when all the stages may be seen amongst one or other of the species:

Pink autumn crocuses spring from the earth while it is still dry, in response to the first drops of rain, and mark the beginning of the winter flowering season.

right: *The rains of November and December bring up the mushrooms, some of them very tasty, such as these.*

the singing of the males, declaring their territorial rights; the carrying of material for building; the nests themselves, with eggs or fledglings and, last but not least, the parents feeding their young outside the nest. Similar activities may be observed among the mammals, although they are shyer in their habits and do not raise their young in full view. At the same time, reptiles leave their winter hiding-places, and insects fill the air.

This is the season of the harvest for several branches of agriculture. The biggest haul from the honey combs is made now, when the honey from the citrus blossom comes in. The hay is generally brought in from the end of March, and in April early barley and wheat are harvested. The harvest in the Negev and the valleys of the north ends in May, continuing on into June in the hills.

The hot season is a time of quiet and harvest. The vineyards and the orchards become heavy with fruit. The loquat (*Eriolotrya japonica*), the first fruit of the season, is on the market stalls by April. The grapes ripen and, together with them or shortly afterwards, other fruits of all kinds. The oranges (*Citrus sinensis*) and grapefruit (*C. maxima*) which graced every table from October until April make way for apricots, plums, grapes and later, pears and apples. The country dries out as it warms up, although the scorching *sharavs* of April and May rarely recur. Temperatures in the mountains remain around 80°F (27°C), and in the lowlands climb to 90° F (32° C). But the temperature alone gives little indication of how people feel. In the more humid areas, for instance along the sea coast, quite moderate temperatures can become almost unbearable, while in the drier parts of the country it is possible to tolerate temperatures which sound appalling to people living in Europe. The early morning hours, when the temperature is rising rapidly and the air is still, are often the most unpleasant time of the day and then, just before noon, a breeze generally springs up and the heat becomes less oppressive.

In June, the sun at noon is at an altitude of 81°, and in Sinai 85°, which is almost directly overhead. Shadows become short and every living creature seeks out some patch of shade. The days lengthen, till they reach fourteen hours of sunshine. Activity, with the exception of sea bathing and the ripening of fruit, declines and the

Foxtail grass—green in spring, yellow in summer — waves us on from season to season.

world of nature sinks into a summer dormancy. Many of the perennials drop their leaves in summer or else shed all their growth above ground, surviving in the form of subterranean bulbs or root stem systems.

With the shortening of the days in September and October there is a change in the air. Clouds begin to gather, and the sunsets take on breathtaking hues. Yet summer is still very much with us and the hottest *sharavs* can be expected about now. The Jews of earlier times used to say that 'the end of summer is harder than the summer.' The olives and the dates ripen and plant life goes through a kind of 'second spring', a short season of budding that seems like a sigh of relief that the arid heat of the summer is over and the refreshing chill of winter is not far off. The landscape is green because those trees that shed their leaves do so later, in December and January.

One day in October the *yoreh* comes suddenly, generally following several days of *sharav* conditions. It never fails to catch everyone unprepared. Every Israeli child knows that the first rain is due any day now, but after half a year in the lightest of summer clothing, and practically living out of doors, the *yoreh* always comes as a surprise. It spells the beginning of the rainy season, but not the end of the heat. It may yet be followed by several weeks of hot clear days, when the farmers look anxiously at the sky and ask each other if winter is ever going to come this year.

This is the time of the main bird migration, when the skies are filled with flocks of migratory birds of different species. The most conspicuous are the white storks and pelicans, but other birds too are well in evidence.

Just as the traditional beginning of the hot season is at Passover, so its conclusion is celebrated at the Festival of Tabernacles, which falls in the middle of the Hebrew month of Tishri (some time in October). The Jewish service now discards the prayer for dew and substitutes the prayer for rain. The year has come full circle.

64

*'Behold now behemoth, which I made with thee;
he eateth grass as an ox.'*

(Job 40:15)

THE NATURAL HISTORY OF THE LAND OF THE PATRIARCHS

As we have already said, the animal and plant life of the land of Israel has not changed very much in the past several thousand years, but while this assertion is basically true it is also a little misleading: to the extent that the presence of man alters nature, it has changed the environment in Israel. The face of the countryside has altered considerably in the past 10,000 or 15,000 years, and even though the changes are to some extent due to the forces of nature, it must be admitted that the activities of man are mainly responsible.

A contemporary who wants to see elephants must either go to the zoo or take a trip to Africa; 15,000 years ago he could have met them face to face in Israel as they browsed among the vegetation at their leisure. Tusks from those days are still to be found, and while they are not polished to the finish to which we are accustomed they are easily identifiable. The bones of elephants which died half a million years ago have been found in the Jordan Valley in a recognizable condition.

There were also many other examples of African wild life to be found here in considerable numbers. The abundant vegetation in the marshes along the coastal plain and in the Jordan Valley was an ideal habitat for beasts like the hippopotamus. Some of them were still there in the fourth millennium BC, and gained their place in recorded history through the accounts of hunting trips which were made by the kings of Mesopotamia. By the time the Old Testament was written such giants were already extinct in this part of the world, and had no place in the surroundings of the ancient Hebrews.

Nevertheless, the Hebrews were acquainted with a number of creatures which can no longer be found in Israel. The cave-homes of the prehistoric inhabitants of the land shed much light on what they ate 40,000 years ago. The caves excavated on Mount Carmel yielded not only the skulls and bones of human beings but also bones left over from thousands of long-forgotten meals. These cavemen used to sit around the fire in the centre of their caverns, gnawing what meat they could off the bones and then tossing the remains over their shoulders against the wall. All along the sides, the archaeologists came upon pile after pile of bones, enough to keep them busy for years in their task of identification and classification.

From their studies, it appears that the cavemen of Carmel lived off scores of different kinds of animals. Some of them would be acceptable fare even today; others not. Some of them are extinct, or at any rate they are in Israel. The forests on the Carmel range, and the swampland which lay between the hills and the sea, were a wonderful breeding ground for these species.

Sycamores survive those who plant them, and even their homes, and may sometimes be found far from present habitation, testifying to the existence of a village on the spot scores or even hundreds of years ago.

The sycamore was a valuable tree in earlier times, when its edible fruits were a common source of food for the poor. The Prophet Amos declared himself to be '...a gatherer of sycamore fruit' as a sign that he was a simple man (7:14).

This half-breed zoo dweller shows traces of the vanished Syrian bears, which lived in the wild in Israel up to a hundred years ago, but are now extinct.

right: *Guarding its tail so care–fully as it sleeps, this fox seems to uphold the ancient tradition of 'Samson's foxes'.*

The wild boar (*Sus scrofa*) had not yet become a forbidden food for the inhabitants of the Holy Land and the Carmel dwellers, who ate their flesh with relish and did not waste their sharp tusks, using them as tools. As a forest animal the Psalmist knew his depredations: 'The boar out of the wood doth waste it . . .' Over the years, these unlovely beasts were systematically hunted down and eventually withdrew into the fastness of the swamps. In the past hundred years they have congregated almost exclusively in the Hula swamp and the thickets lining the Jordan River, from whence they set out for the cultivated lands on their missions of pillage and destruction. With the draining of the swamps in recent years, the boars have returned to their first home, the woods.

Another woodland beast which held its own on Mount Carmel until this century was the Carmel roe deer (*Capreolus capreolus*). It was an animal similar to its European relatives, but the buck grew only small, three-pointed, antlers. It lived among the thickets and trees, but as the forests increasingly fell prey to the woodman's axe it fled from vanishing grove to vanishing grove. Although the deer was the emblem of the Tribe of Naphtali ('Naphtali is a hind let loose'), whose land was the hill country overlooking the Hula Valley in the north, it had moved south centuries earlier, and was to be found only on Mount Carmel. It was the deer's misfortune that it was not only beautiful but also tasty, and thus sought after by mountain hunters and city gluttons alike. The last deer was killed at the beginning of this century, and the country lost one of its most interesting species.

The Persian fallow deer (*Dama mesopotamica*) also figured on the menu of our cavemen, but it disappeared long before the roe deer. Apparently man was not entirely to blame. Investigators who examined the piles of bones discovered that remains of fallow deer grew more and more rare towards the upper levels, corresponding to changes in the climate of the country. Presumably, as their survival became more precarious, men ate the few that remained.

An exotic neighbour of the roe deer and the fallow deer was the Nile crocodile (*Crocodilus niloticus*), which made its home in the swamps lying between the Carmel range and the sea. The separation of Israel and the African continent occurred in the very distant past, but the little enclave at the foot of Mount Carmel remained for many more thousands of years, providing an agreeable habitat for this crocodile which is now confined to Africa. Despite the density of the population in this area during Roman times, as well as the proximity of Caesarea, one of the largest cities of antiquity, the crocodiles held their own, and a city, Crocodilopolis, on the banks of a nearby stream, was even named after them. The name, as well as the animals whose presence it recorded, was preserved in later days despite changes in population. The Arabs called the stream Timsakh, which is crocodile in Arabic. The reptiles themselves could still be found up to the middle of the nineteenth century. Only then were the last two hunted down, and the species vanished from the land.

Let us now return to the ruminants. When the Bible was written there were still plenty of them, belonging to various species. They were of special interest, as only . . . 'every beast that parteth the hoof, and cleaveth the cleft into two claws, and cheweth the cud among the beasts, that ye shall eat.' (Deuteronomy 14: 6). Of these, Moses named seven wild animals, as well as three domestic ones. All ten are listed in Deuteronomy 14: 5–6, and at least three more, belonging to the same group, are mentioned elsewhere. The translation of their names in the Authorized Version is not of great help to us. Even Jewish scholars of the Talmud did not know exactly what each one was, and contemporary scientists can identify with certainty only half of the species. Only two, the gazelle and the ibex, have survived in the wild in Israel, and they will be discussed later. Some of the animals, the wild goat (*Capra hircus aegargus*) and the Persian fallow deer, were to be found in the surrounding area and, at the beginning of the century, could still be met within the historical boundaries of the Land of Israel, chiefly in the Syrian desert, but unrestricted hunting has since wiped out those that were left.

It might be worth mentioning one of the others, the oryx (*Oryx leucoryx*), a kind of antelope, which is apparently the Hebrew *re'em* of the Bible and the unicorn of the Authorized Version: 'But my horn shalt thou exalt like the horn of an unicorn: I shall be anointed with fresh oil.' (Psalms 92: 10). Descriptions of the unicorn, again and again, stress its horn as its most striking feature, and the long straight horns of the oryx, which can attain as much as a yard in length, fit these descriptions best. The idea of a one-horned animal may have arisen from an optical illusion when looking at an oryx in profile, or from one such beast maimed in a fight. Several species of this genus still roam the wilds of Africa, though the biblical oryx was apparently a species which until quite recently used to inhabit the Arabian peninsula, but which has now almost disappeared as a result of indiscriminate hunting. In the

The cheetah survived in remote areas on the fringe of the desert until the end of the 19th century, but is no longer to be seen in the wild in Israel.

'*Pariah dogs*' *were regarded until recently as inferior, but their many qualities have now been recognized and the breed has been renamed* '*Canaanite dog*'.

right: *Sheep grazing beneath ancient olive trees still look much as they must have done to the Patriarchs and Prophets of old.*

course of this century, it was thought that the oryx was becoming extinct. They had become so rare that a few years ago a pair fetched $25,000 (£8,500).

The wild sheep and the wild goat no longer adorn the landscape of Israel, but if their domesticated descendants, less well equipped for the war of survival, are able to graze in their thousands on the hills of the country, there is no reason to believe that their wild forbears did not prosper here in the ages before the coming of man.

The beast of prey which made the deepest impression on the ancients — not only the Hebrews — was of course the lion (*Panthera leo*). They are mentioned scores of times in the Bible, and not under one name but under six. Their significance may be lost in translation but they each carry a different connotation in Hebrew. They are *aryeh, ari, k'fir, lavi, laish* and *shahal*. It is expressed most wonderfully in the Book of Job, where some of the best descriptions of the wild life of this country are to be found. In two sentences (Job 4: 10–11) the writer uses five different names, for which the translator was forced to use the one word 'lion' five times. This alone, as well as the large number of extant carvings, drawings and images from the time, testifies to the fact that the lion was a very real presence in the ancient Land of Israel and that it did not confine itself to the deserts but prowled through the very heart of the country.

Those who wish to see the lion of Judah must now travel to the wild life sanctuaries of Africa, where they may encounter just such a lioness with her cub. Lions were exterminated in Israel some eight hundred years ago.

below: *The leopard cannot rest as peacefully in Israel as it does in the African nature reserves. Here they are rare and seldom seen, last survivors of the large beasts of prey.*

above: *The ox and the ass perform the ancient rite of threshing, as they have since the dawn of agriculture: but not for much longer, as machines move in to take their place.*

Mother and son; they care not that men take their name to call each other 'donkey'.

The baby fawn is soon strong enough to run in the wild and follow its mother. The mother gazelle leaves her fawn for some days after birth, watching from a distance and coming every few hours to give suck.

below: *Although the porcupine is strictly nocturnal in habit, spending its days in the burrow which it excavates with its strong claws, it is well known for the damage it causes in vegetable gardens, and because of the black and white spines which it sheds.*

Besides the many places where lions are mentioned specifically in the Bible, there are some stories of actual encounters between lion and man, all in settled areas. Most famous, of course, is Samson's lion (Judges 14). When the hero was in the vineyards of Timnah, on his way to visit his bride, a young lion roared at him. It must have been fairly well grown, or its mother would have been nearby, in which case Samson's plight would indeed have been a sorry one. Even so, such an encounter could have meant a sad end for anyone else, but Samson came out of it as victor. 'He rent him as he would have rent a kid', and did not even bother to tell his parents about his brave deed. Out of the carcass of that lion came not only honey, but also the story of Samson's famous riddle and its solution.

Another graphic account tells how David, the young shepherd, boasted of killing a lion single-handed, when he asked permission to go and fight Goliath (I Samuel 17: 34–36). His method of dealing with the lion was somewhat different from Samson's. He caught his lion by the head, and smote him and killed him. No wonder that when he became a king one of his heroes was distinguished for having killed a lion: Benaiah, son of Jehoiada, went down and slew a lion in the midst of a pit in time of snow (II Samuel 23: 20). Yet another lion became famous for executing the will of God. When the Man of God, sent to prophesy against Jeroboam, broke God's command by taking food at Beth-el (I Kings 13), a lion was sent to punish him, and slew him on the way between Beth-el (the village now known as Beitin, north-east of Ramallah) and Jerusalem. It did not touch the man's ass, and so were they found: the body of the Man of God lying in the path, and the ass and the lion standing by it.

The war between man and the lion lasted a long time. Despite the spread of permanent settlements, and despite the hunting parties arranged by kings and nobles, lions still roamed the land 2,000 years after Samson and David. From records which have come down to us it appears that the last lions were killed about 800 years ago, during the Crusades, but even after their extinction their mark remained in literature, art, thought and even in the names of people. One of the more noble examples is the title of Lion of Judah, borne by the Emperor of Ethiopia. The same lion of Judah also serves as the emblem of the City of Jerusalem.

Another representative of the cat family is the leopard (*Panthera pardus*), which may still be found in Israel. Contrary to popular belief, tigers never lived here, and the Bible does not speak of tigers, but of leopards, specifically mentioning the 'leopard's spots'. In contrast to the lion, which makes its home in the wide open spaces of the steppe, the leopard is a forest dweller, a denizen of closed-in places, and far more circumspect in its relations with man. It probably owes its survival to this caution. Even now, hardly a year passes without some report of a leopard being seen in the forests of Galilee, and every once in a while hunters manage to kill one.

In recent times, a desert leopard has been reliably identified in the Judean wilderness. It is smaller than its forest relative and has acquired desert habits.

Another cat which, while it may not have been mentioned in the Bible, almost certainly existed in this part of the world in biblical times is the cheetah (*Acinonyx jubatus*). The last ones were seen in the eastern deserts of the Land of Israel at the end of the last century and the beginning of the twentieth, and optimists among animal lovers would not be surprised to find them still, in the deserts of the Arava and Sinai.

The beast of prey next most feared after the lion was the bear. Like the lion, it also made no effort to avoid settled areas, and the farmers and shepherds of antiquity were well acquainted with them. As far as we can tell, the bear of the Bible is the Syrian bear (*Ursus syriacus*), and Israel represented the southern extreme of its distribution. The species was quite light in colour. Today there are no pure-bred animals of this species alive, even in zoos. This bear survived here in the wild longer than the lion, and one was seen in the 1860's in Nahal Amud, near the Sea of Galilee, by the British naturalist Tristram. At the beginning of the twentieth century, the celebrated naturalist Aharoni took part in a bear hunt in southern Lebanon. Since then there have been no reliable reports of the presence of bears. Among Jews the names Arie (lion), Dov (bear) and Ze'ev (wolf) are quite common, even today, and similar names are found among Arabs too.

Together with some beasts of the field, at least one large bird, the ostrich (*Struthio camelus*), has disappeared from the biblical landscape. It is mentioned several times in the Bible, and is held up as an example of stupidity in a lively passage in Job (39: 13–18). The ostrich's eggs, which served our forefathers as containers and as charms, are today on display in many museums, and ornamentations deriving from their plumage are represented in ancient pictures. They used to inhabit the deserts of southern and eastern Israel, but were hunted to extinction in these regions for their feathers. The last indigenous ostriches were captured at the end of last century, and this species can now be found only in the plains of Africa.

If we add to the list of animals which have disappeared the names of those which still remain, we get a picture of a country rich in wild life. How did it come to be so much reduced? The Land of Israel has been settled by civilized man since time immemorial. The first strata of ancient Jericho date back to the sixth millennium BC; there were farming communities in the Jordan basin 10,000 years ago and, in the Jezreel Valley, villages exist today which still bear the names they had 4,000 years ago. A dense and active population in such a small country inevitably left its mark on nature. Even without man the last 15,000 years have witnessed climatic changes; swamps have dried up, forests have shrunk and the steppelands have spread, all in their turn affecting the prehistoric wild life even though, to the best of our knowledge, the temperatures and rain precipitation in this area have remained unchanged in

A wasps' nest; trap for the un-wary. The insects, though small, can leave a sharp and painful sting.

recorded time and the animals which inhabited the land as long as 5,000 years ago would have no trouble in making themselves at home here today. Their fate was decided by the spread of civilization.

The process of change and destruction ran in cycles which have recurred several times in the history of the country. In the beginning there was a primeval landscape, and man entered the picture only as a hunter. He had practically no effect on plant life and his depredations upon the animal kingdom were marginal. As he settled down and took to farming he began to clear away the wild vegetation, at first from the heavy soil in the valleys, afterwards on the soft chalk hills and finally on the harder limestone slopes. His cultivated lowland fields and his terraces planted with grain encroached upon the natural vegetation. The first such cycle reached its climax in the time of the kingdoms of Judea and Israel, about 1,000 to 600 BC, with an intricate system of terracing, mountain orchards and irrigated crops. The soil, which until then had been retained by natural forest, was now preserved from erosion by man-made stone terraces and the daily care lavished upon it by the Hebrew farmers.

The jungle cat, almost exterminated when its natural habitat was drained, has found a new lease of life around the fishponds.

right: *A small pool in the Hula nature reserve, surrounded by water plants, providing a glimpse of the landscape of the swamp, much as it may have been for thousands of years.*

The wooden plough, as still used by the Arab peasants, has not changed for centuries, though modern machines threaten to replace it.

Wild wheat, from which modern hard wheat strains have been developed, still waves on the mountain slopes of Judea and Galilee.

Wars and destruction brought this period of history to an end. The trees were cut down for use during siege, the orchards were burned down and the farmers were either killed or exiled. The land and the terraces were neglected and fell into ruin. The soil was eroded and the vineyards which remained were allowed to die. The hills now had neither their original covering of forest trees nor the cultivated plantations which replaced them. Normally, the original vegetation would have reasserted itself, but now there was not enough soil to support it, and the process of creating new soil is a long one. The trees returned, but very slowly.

Eventually a new wave of settlement spread over the land during the time of the Jewish commonwealth of the Second Temple (516 BC–AD 70). Terraces appeared on the hillsides once more, trees were planted and the land cared for. Once again, the natural vegetation was banished. Eventually another war, and sometimes several wars in close succession, brought new waves of destruction. The countryside was violated in this way countless times, and over the generations hardly any part of it escaped desolation at one time or another. The land reached its lowest ebb during the second half of the nineteenth century, both in terms of its natural setting and its population. What little was left of its former beauty could only give a faint suggestion of the riches that once had been.

From a first glance at the barren, rock-ribbed hillside you might say that the stories of thick forests were only the imaginary embellishment so common to the legends of antiquity, but apart from the documentary evidence which we have, starting with the Pharaohs and right down to modern times, the most important evidence is on the spot for all to see: some of the giant trees themselves have somehow survived the general destruction and stand in solitary state next to the grave of some Moslem holy man, to bear living witness to the forests as once they were.

Deciduous trees hide their age in summer beneath a thick cloak of green leaves, but in winter the truth is revealed in the thick branches and wrinkled bark.

The practice of tree worship was common in the Land of Israel from ancient times. The Hebrew names of both the oak and the terebinth (*allon* and *elah*) contain the Canaanite word *el*, meaning God. Both are long-lived, some of them reaching ages of more than 1,000 years. With their vast branches sprouting out of thick virile trunks, and the marks of age, with semblances of human faces and limbs on them, it was not difficult to believe in their supernatural powers. The Torah (the Law) does not mince words in condemning these idolatrous practices, and in no less than sixteen places mentions the altars 'upon every high hill and under every green tree.' Popular belief among the Moslems made the ancient tombs, superstitiously laid near trees, into the burial places of Islamic prophets, and magical powers were attributed to these venerable trees, which were often held to be so sacred that whoever dared to violate them would surely be punished.

Spared in this way were impressive oaks, terebinths, zizyphus, sycamores and others. Sometimes they are not completely isolated, but survive in groups or even in forests, like the preserve of Atlantic terebinths (*Pistacia atlantica*) at Ein Avazim in upper Galilee or the magnificent oaks at the Tal Grove, near the headwaters of the Jordan. With the aid of these few examples we can imagine what the land looked like in ancient times.

From the beginning of modern Jewish settlement in Palestine, a determined effort has been made to restore the country's fertility and make it once again a green and pleasant land, rich in trees and in animal life. Thousands of acres of the mountain slopes have been planted with forest trees, mostly pine, and laws have been passed to protect wild life. Nature reserves have been defined to retain the primeval qualities of particular areas, whether woodland, swamp or desert. Some of the landscape and animals of biblical times can never be restored to their original state, but much of what the Bible describes is again there to be seen.

'The wilderness and the solitary place shall be glad for them; and the desert shall rejoice, and blossom as the rose.'

(Isaiah 35:1)

A desert animal may hide, but the footprints it leaves in the night will be there to be read in the morning.

THE DESERT SHALL REJOICE

The very word desert conjures up visions of endless wastes of sand, blinding storms, areas of quicksand, and the whitening bones of camels fallen by the way. The deserts of Israel are as different from this popular conception as it is possible to be, both in appearance and in character, consisting mostly of rocky hills and not 'wastes of sand', though these are there as well. (In Arabic the word *sakhra*, from which the Sahara derives its name, means 'rock', indicating a desert of stones and not sand.)

The common Hebrew word for desert, *midbar*, means literally a grazing land for flocks, and not necessarily a desolate wilderness. Occasionally we find the word *midbar* linked in the Bible with the name of a settlement, such as Midbar Zif, or Midbar Ma'on, meaning the grazing ground of the village of Zif or Ma'on. To indicate an absolute wilderness, the ancient Hebrew would use the words *tsia* or *yeshimon*, which are generally translated as wasteland and desolation.

We have already referred to the fact that the deserts of southern and eastern Israel are climatic wildernesses. It is neither the composition of the soil nor any other factor connected with the lie of the land which makes it barren, but solely the absence of water. There is no basic difference in the origin, geological structure or chemistry of the limestone hills of the Negev and Judea and those of the Mount Carmel range and Galilee, and whatever differences there are in the soil can be attributed to the climate; areas of heavy rainfall evolve soils different from those in arid areas.

Another argument in support of our contention may be found in those places where desert and water meet, in the oases. Here, the vegetation shows no sign that

left: *Rainwater, gathering in a crevice amongst the rocks of the desert, which will serve as a natural reservoir even in the summer months.*

The desert monitor, whose Hebrew name means strength; and strength it has, in its tail and in its mouth. Woe to any rat between its sharp teeth!

the soil is inhospitable. Rather the contrary is true; if water is available, the supposedly barren soil of the desert will support even the most delicate plant life. The oases of Jericho and Ein Gedi were famous in antiquity, and in our own time Jewish settlements established on the indisputably desert shores of the Dead Sea and in the Arava have managed to develop a flourishing agriculture through land irrigation. So we see that there is no sharp division between the desert and cultivable land. In this part of the Middle East the farmer has fought an unceasing struggle with the desert since earliest times. As civilization advanced man penetrated deeper into the wilderness, and developed methods of cultivation, water storage and building suited to his surroundings. Cisterns were dug, and a system of ditches laid out to channel whatever precipitation there was into them for storage. The ravines were dammed by a series of terraces, to trap the soil which was washed down with the water from the hillsides. Fields and orchards, houses and terraces advanced into the desert.

Then the desert retaliated. Tribes of nomads with their flocks, and armed raiders, emerged from the desert to destroy the fields and the gardens; the frontier of cultivation was pushed back once more and the cycle began again. The remains of hundreds of villages, large and small, can be found scattered throughout the deserts of Israel. They had their day and then reverted to desert once more. Among them are six cities dating back to the Byzantine period, as well as many relics of the reigns of the Kings of Judah — roads, fortresses, terraces and cisterns.

The desert here is unlike the Sahara, with its sandy wastes; rather is it a broad expanse of stone and rock, with occasional stretches of sand. In the northern part of Sinai there is sand, as well as a little in the west; the rest of the peninsula is rocky. In the south and near Eilat there is granite, and sandstone of many colours, and throughout most of the Negev and Judea chalk and limestone.

The *midbar* of Israel does not resemble the desert of the south-western United States and Mexico. There the desert is watered by at least ten inches of rain a year.

Camels in their natural habitat in the Judean Desert: a white female is rare.

In Israel, this much rain is sufficient to grow barley. But the principal difference lies in the vegetation. In Israel there are none of the succulent plants, the cacti, which lend to the American desert its special character. None of this group, nor anything resembling it, can be found here.

An annual precipitation of eight inches will support a thin layer of vegetation, low bushes and grasses, even in places where water never flows. In special conditions, even trees will strike root and grow and, when they do, they attain a size and age worthy of any forest. In the Negev uplands, 3,200 feet above sea level, there are several hundred Atlantic terebinths (*Pistacia atlantica*). This tree occurs over a wide area, from the Atlas Mountains of North Africa in the west to the steppes of the Middle East, with vast deserts separating one patch of trees from the next. Some of those in the Negev are many hundreds of years old and it would be no exaggeration to say that, amongst those still standing, some were already there at the period of the Second Temple, or, in other words, from the time of Jesus. A trunk with a girth of as much as twenty feet is not unusual. Despite their age the trees still spring into new life every year, their leaves red in bud, green in their prime and red again at the fall.

The granite gorges of Sinai, and the Negev near Eilat, change colour with every hour of the day according to the intensity and direction of the sun's rays.

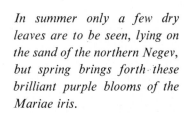

In summer only a few dry leaves are to be seen, lying on the sand of the northern Negev, but spring brings forth these brilliant purple blooms of the Mariae iris.

A large corm, deep in the loess soil, supports this fine display of broad green leaves and cone of yellow flowerets — the lion's leaf.

The shores of the Dead Sea belie its name: camels graze among the low shrubs, and the thorny acacia tree adds a brilliant touch of green.

below: *Despite its fearsome appearance, the big and clumsy dabb-lizard, 'crocodile of the desert', is a harmless vegetarian disappearing into its hole at the slightest suspicious sound or movement.*

right: *A recent discovery in the Negev, the Spafford Sternbergia was formerly regarded as a typical flower of the Mediterranean zone.*

A pool of pure ice-cold water, fed by a small spring, and a narrow water-fall — hidden among the rocks — in the Wilderness of Zin, in the Negev.

Where the rainfall is less than four to six inches in a year, the region becomes a true desert. Nothing then will grow, except in the ravines or in some other depression, where whatever moisture falls can collect and so support life. When looking at such barren wastes, it is hard to imagine the force and violence of the flash floods that occur in these areas every year. The minimal amounts of rainfall are not spaced out over the winter, but descend in sudden storms at intervals of weeks or months, between October and May. The dry river beds are long, draining large tracts of arid country where the soil does not absorb water. Rain, which in the north of the country would barely be enough to moisten the upper level of the soil, collects here in tiny rivulets which flow down into the principal ravines to become raging torrents that sweep away everything lying in their path — trees, boulders and flocks. The flow lasts for several hours, stopping as suddenly as it began. The passage in Job (6: 15) 'My brethren have dealt deceitfully as a brook, and as the stream of brooks they pass away' and in the Psalms (126: 4) 'Turn again our captivity, O Lord, as the streams in the south' are illuminated afresh for anyone seeing for the first time a flash flood in the Negev. Some of the flood waters are absorbed into the beds of the ravines and nourish the plant life that subsists there.

There is only one short growing season in the desert, lasting a month or two during a dry year and up to five months if the rains are bountiful. During the rest of the year the desert is bone dry, with chill nights and burning hot days.

Botany textbooks devote considerable space to some of the remarkable means which have been devised by nature so that plants can survive under such conditions. We will describe only a few. The basic principle is the same in every case; as they cannot live in the normal way they have all evolved some special survival technique.

Some concentrate their entire life span into a short growing season and just vanish when the hot dry season begins. The simplest method is that of the annuals. The life cycle in the desert is rapid. It takes only a few months for the plant to germinate, grow leaves, blossom, ripen its seeds and then to wither. All its efforts are bent upon one objective; to flower and bear fruit, even at the expense of its own existence. Thus you see tiny, almost unformed plants, with only two or three leaves, bravely putting forth their flowers. In a good year, the plants produce seeds for several seasons ahead. Some of them will germinate only some years hence, some will germinate during the following year and survive, and others will be tempted too soon by a few drops of moisture, only to parch to death when water fails.

The geophytes (bulbous plants) behave in much the same way. During a good year they support green leaves and bloom and when the dry season comes they do not disappear entirely, but shed only their growth above the surface, storing their nourishment in the bulb in the depths of the ground. Some of the most splendid flowering bulbs to be found in Israel, such as the Negev iris and the Negev tulip,

Far away in the dry ravines of the central Negev there are scores of terebinths. Able to survive a number of years of continuous drought, they live to a great age. The massive terebinth (left) *on a high mountain in the Negev may be more than a thousand years old: to judge by the wrinkles on its ancient trunk it surely has many a story to tell.*

the corn lily (*Ixiolirion*) and the yellow star flowers (*Sternbergia*), grow in the steppe regions, but the further we penetrate into the true desert the fewer the geophytes become and, by the time we reach Eilat, there are no more to be found.

The deciduous plants of the desert also follow the principle of conserving their strength during the dry season. As opposed to the accepted plant rhythm in the temperate regions, they shed their leaves in summer rather than at the onset of winter. The falling of the leaves is caused, not by the cold and the snow but by the heat and the dryness, and thus some plants and shrubs are green and fresh throughout the winter, but are bare during the summer months. Non-deciduous plants drastically reduce the surface area of their leaves, and thus cut down water loss through evaporation. Either they put forth smaller narrower leaves or else transfer the function of the leaves to the stem, as in the white broom.

There are also plants which are active the whole year round, and indeed some which are at their peak in the hot arid months. They draw the water they need from the parched land in one of three ways. Some build up extremely high osmotic pressure, to enable them to extract the last drop of moisture from the soil. Others either put down roots deep enough to tap subterranean sources or cast them widely enough to capture every available drop of surface water, including dew.

This explains how trees can survive in the desert, and even reach a very considerable size. This is especially true of the acacia (*Acacia* spp.), which made such a deep impression on the Children of Israel after the Exodus from Egypt. When

Moses came to build the Ark of the Covenant and the Tabernacle and needed beams and timber it was only natural that he should turn to the acacia, shittim in the Bible (Exodus 25 and 26). There are three principal species of this picturesque tree. One is tall, with branches emanating from the main trunk. The other two have a number of trunks, rising out of the ground like a fan. Some of them live for hundreds of years and their leaves are an important source of nourishment for many animals, among them the gazelle and the camel.

Another group of plants are parasites. There are not many, only a few all told, but these few are colourful and catch the eye. The enormous effort expended by the host plant in collecting each drop of water is of absolutely no concern to the parasites. They waste the precious fluid in lavish display. The most striking among them is the acacia mistletoe, which attaches itself to various bushes and trees. It has fresh green leaves and its abundant red flowers are a centre of attraction for birds and insects. Another desert parasite is the broom-rape (*Orobranche*), which draws its nourishment from the roots of the tamarisk (*Tamarix articulata*). Its yellow or violet flowers can grow as much as twenty inches high.

The desert reaches the peak of its beauty when it bursts into bloom, in every colour and on every side, between February and the beginning of April. In terms of quantity, the endless living carpets of the northern Negev take pride of place; sprinkled with white and purple, their fragrance sweetens the very air from Beersheba to the north. In the western Negev, the groundsels and dandelions turn vast areas into seas of golden yellow, splashed with little islands of pastel-tinted flowers of different hues.

At the same time the white broom (*Retama*), with its fragrant blossom, comes to life along the dry beds of the ravines, with deep purple irises at its feet and brilliant red Negev tulips along the hillsides up above, while crimson anemones (*Anemone coronaria*) flower among the rocks and with them scarlet buttercups (*Ranunculus asiaticus*). The desert in bloom is an unforgettable sight, revealing to the full the imagery of those verses in the Bible in which the prophet or the poet expresses his elation at the sight or recollection of the wilderness in flower.

To the casual observer, the desert appears to be completely devoid of living things, but just as the impression that it is barren of plants is mistaken, so it will be found that animal life is not lacking. If you take a good look at some sandy patch, or a stretch of soft soil, you will see tracks, of various sizes, which can only denote the presence of animals. Of course these desert dwellers will not put in an appearance at the hours most convenient to man. They have their own problems of survival and their own ways of adjusting to prevailing conditions. For the most part the animals cannot emulate the plants, which survive the difficult season as seeds, or in a dormant state. Nevertheless, some of the desert creatures practise aestivation (summer dormancy). Good examples are the various species of snail which are scattered

Granite mountains of Sinai; perhaps the two
tablets containing the ten commandments were
hewn from among these rocks.

throughout the desert. They are active only in winter, and in summer close the openings of their sparkling white shells with a layer of chalk and go to sleep. Their dormant state does not put off the desert mice in the least. The spiny-mouse (*Acomys cahrinus*) and the gerbils (*Gerbillus*) take the snails to their burrows, where they break open the shells and devour the inmates while they are still asleep. You can always spot a mouse hole from a distance by the pile of snails' shells deposited outside.

Mice, which are active throughout the year, face a problem which is shared by all the animals in the desert: how to conserve water. How do these creatures find the water they need to live, and how do they use it in the most effective way? The gazelle and the ibex can wander at will, even in the summer months, in search of distant water holes. The mice do not enjoy this degree of mobility, yet they thrive in the very heart of the desert, far from any source of water. It appears that they obtain the fluids they need from their food, without drinking so much as a single drop of water for months on end. They extract the maximum use from their body fluids and hardly any is excreted.

The mouse is only one of a number of animals which have developed special ways of survival in the desert. For example, the gazelle can also survive for weeks without water, deriving whatever fluid it needs from the grass it grazes on.

Animals cannot hope to change the desert and they cannot always adapt themselves to its capricious ways, although they generally seem to find a place in the empty expanses where they can subsist and raise their young, either in a burrow in the ground or among the rocks, in a crack under a stone or just in a patch of shade. In the heart of the parched and scorching wilderness, the animals find themselves some nook which is just a little cooler, a little damper and a little shadier; a place where they can take cover during those hours, and even days, when they would prefer not to be abroad under the burning sun. Beneath every stone in the desert you can uncover a teeming community of which there is not a hint on the barren surface.

For the most part, the desert animals tend to be coloured black, or else the yellow-brown of their environment. Zoologists have not arrived at any satisfactory explanation for the black. One theory holds that the colour serves as a mark of identification for creatures which are interested in finding one another, such as the black desert ravens (*Corvus corax*). Another claims that it serves as a warning to other animals, as in the case of the poisonous black grasshopper, whose only defences are its colour and its poisonous secretions; the desert-dwellers are all familiar with it, and steer clear. The yellow-brown is of course much more common, serving scores of mammals, birds and insects as camouflage to conceal them from the eyes of their potential enemies.

left: The Wilderness of Zin figures large in the story of the desert wanderings of the Children of Israel. It is difficult to identify the ancient location with certainty, but it is most probably in the valley known by this name today.

above: The sands of the desert, parched and inhospitable, provide the favourite haunt of the absinth shrub, which manages to find all the moisture it needs for survival.

Still only a fledgling, in full growth it will be a cream-coloured courser.

The reptiles have probably made the best adaptation to desert life and we shall deal with them at length in a chapter to themselves. Let it suffice here to say that of the seven species of poisonous snake found in Israel only one makes its home in the north. The others inhabit the sparsely populated Negev and other deserts. The desert abounds with many species of lizards, harduns and geckos, which divide up the territory with almost human logic. Deserving of special attention is the desert monitor (*Varanus*), an inhabitant of the northern Negev, which reaches a length of forty inches. It lives off such little creatures as mice, which it captures and devours with great relish. Then there is the Egyptian dabb-lizard (*Uromastyx aegypticus*) which, in contrast to most other reptiles, is vegetarian. It grows to twenty or twenty-five inches in length and, with its comparatively long legs, thick tail and the yellow colouring which it assumes during the hottest hours of the day, is enough to terrify the unwary hiker, though needlessly. It would not harm a fly. Its rare and magnificently tinted relative, the ornate dabb-lizard, is one of the most beautiful creatures in Israel.

It looks as though the desert must be an ideal place for reptiles. About half the total number of reptilian species known in Israel prosper in the Negev — from the tiny Stendner's gecko (two and a half inches long) to the big monitor. The lizards darting over the rocks and on the sand in springtime are a pleasing sight for the traveller. One cannot say the same of snakes, and especially of the poisonous ones. To the layman it does not matter whether he sees a carpet viper, a horned viper (*Pseudocerastes fieldi*) or a desert cobra; none of them are his friends. His only concern is, which ones are the most dangerous. Fortunately, there are no recorded cases of fatal snake-bites in the desert, but perhaps the Palestinian horned viper is the nastiest to encounter. One of its small relatives generally lies buried in the sand, with only its two vicious-looking eyes peeping out. 'Dan shall be a serpent by the way, an adder in the path, that biteth the horse heels, so that his rider shall fall backwards.' (Genesis 49: 17).

The awe in which these snakes were held led to the story of the serpent of brass. When the people of Israel spoke against God and against Moses, the Lord 'sent fiery serpents that bit the people, and much people died.' As a sort of antidote, Moses set up a serpent of brass on a pole and any man bitten by a snake, who beheld it, lived (Numbers 21: 6–9). This brazen serpent was preserved for hundreds of years as a sacred relic, until King Hezekiah broke it into pieces (II Kings 18: 4).

The traveller in the desert may be surprised to see a duck swimming on a small pond in the heart of the barren wastes. This is not a mirage, but a fact, although the duck will not be a permanent inhabitant of the area. It is just one of the myriads of migratory birds, of different species, which traverse the desert on their north-south route. In springtime it is quite a sight to look up at the soaring birds of prey along the

Caravan routes do not change, though those who travel them may differ in the course of generations. Here a line of young hikers wends its way along an ancient path.

valleys of the Arava, when eagles, vultures, buzzards and hawks share the sky with storks and pelicans, as well as smaller birds.

Apart from the migrants there are, of course, the real desert residents, from the kingly vultures — the bearded, the lappet-faced and the griffon — to the tiny scrub warblers. Around the carcass of a camel one can see a variety of birds, from vultures to ravens, coming from unbelievable distances to gather at the feast. A vulture, hungry for days, can consume so much meat, given an opportunity, that it will not be able to fly for hours.

The lappet-faced vultures (*Torgos tracheliotus*) used to build their huge nests, more than a yard in diameter, in the tops of the acacia trees. In former years there were scores of such nests scattered over the desert, but now a single one will cause a sensation amongst bird-watchers.

Desert vegetation may look like tinder in summer, but when the rains come this 'dead' wood will show itself to be a flourishing bush.

The black ravens (*Corvus corax*) are an inseparable part of the desert scene. The fan-tailed ravens (*C. rhipidurus*) near the Dead Sea and Eilat live in groups, and are bold enough to come as close to human habitation as possible. The big ravens of the inner desert, which are more handsome, usually live in pairs, and keep their distance from man. Such a pair, perched on a low ridge, might sometimes be taken for two old Bedouins. They have been identified with God's messengers, who fed the Prophet Elijah when he hid in the desert.

We must leave the other birds of the desert, however worthy of mention, and take a look at the mammals. Since they will also be considered in a later chapter, we shall confine ourselves at this point to a few brief remarks. Unlike the reptiles, which can go for weeks without food, a mammal must eat (and sometimes drink) regularly, which makes life in the desert quite difficult. One may be convinced, although not easily, that the vegetarians can manage to find enough nourishment from the almost non-existent vegetation, by the simple fact that these animals are there to be seen. But what of the carnivores? How does a fox or a desert cat get its food? Certainly they must have keen senses and a very good knowledge of their environment, or else the ability to range over great distances in search of food. They are both agile and cautious, and although each species is represented by only limited numbers, yet they survive.

Life on the verge of the desert made a great impression on the people of the Bible. In spite of the popular notion, it is not in the Pentateuch that the features of the desert are best described. The Book of Job, for instance, conveys the true atmosphere of the desert. Many passages in this book, and even its underlying ideas, were misunderstood, or wrongly translated, because the interpreters failed to visualize them in their desert context. The same is true of passages in other books of the Bible.

'But ye, O mountains of Israel, ye shall shoot forth your branches, and yield your fruit to my people of Israel...'

(Ezekiel 36:8)

The Mount Tabor oak supplies goats with a feast of acorns at the end of summer. Botanists also value these, as a means of distinguishing this species from other closely-related oaks.

GET THEE UP TO THE WOOD COUNTRY

On reviewing the chronicles of the Crusades we find an interesting reference to a forest in Wadi Felik, near Arsuf. It comes in an account of a battle between the armies of Richard Lionheart and Saladin, when the former was advancing along the coast from Acre to Jaffa. Saladin decided to attack the Crusaders at this point, where there was a well-grown forest, one mile wide and twelve miles long, covering the mountain slopes and coming down within two miles of the seashore. Richard's army had to pass this way (5–7 September 1191) and the king, knowing of the forest, expected the Saracens to lie in wait for him there. The Saracens concealed themselves in the middle of the forest, waiting for the Crusaders to pass through the open land, and pounced out upon them from the trees. The whole area between the road and the forest was suddenly filled with well-organized Saracen forces. The Crusaders withstood three attacks before the Saracens withdrew into the forest, and Richard returned with his army to Arsuf.

Wadi Felik and Arsuf are easy enough to find, and anyone who feels like it can follow King Richard's line of march. One thing only is missing: the forest. But a good botanist will be able to point to traces of it here and there; perhaps a lone small oak tree, or some forest creeper. The forest itself has disappeared, but there can be no doubt of its existence, even long before the time of the Crusaders. It was also described by Josephus Flavius, a historian of the 1st century AD, who wrote of a battle which was fought in the woodland on this spot about a hundred years before his own time.

The combination of rocks, trees and water is one in which man finds inspiration everywhere in the world.

Running water and forest trees are not a common sight in Israel, even in Galilee, where fresh water springs are comparatively abundant.

A more recent anecdote brings the story of the destruction of the forests closer to our day. It tells of an old Arab sheikh, only two generations ago, who used, in his youth, to ride to Jaffa through the woodland in the Sharon. In the course of time he became blind and rode no more, but in his old age he asked his son to take him to Jaffa once again. As they passed through this area, the son saw his father bending low on his ass. When he asked why, the answer the old man gave was that he wanted to dodge the branches of the big trees. The trees he remembered no longer existed: they had been cut down by the Turks.

This is not the only forest in Israel which once was and is no more. Travellers in the last century and early Jewish settlers alike were astonished by the parched barrenness of the land. This may seem strange to us today, when we look at the hundreds of thousands of acres of well-watered countryside, with fields, orchards and woods where they saw only parched yellow-brown wastes. The destruction of the old forests reached its peak during the First World War, when the Turks needed fuel for their locomotives: in the absence of coal they cut down whole forests for burning. The woodland we see today is partly a regrowth of those forests, with stretches of the original which escaped the axe, and partly new afforestation carried out in recent decades.

The natural woodland still remaining in Israel amounts to a total of about a hundred thousand acres, in Galilee, on the Mount Carmel range, in the Jerusalem hills and on the heights of Golan and Gilead. Remnants of the old forest can also be seen in the form of solitary trees and small clumps, scattered widely over the countryside. From these, together with the historical evidence, it is possible to arrive at some idea of what the country's forest land may have been like in ancient times. Woodland covered almost all the country in those days, with many tall trees of great age.

It can be assumed that the forests flourished best in the deep soil of the valleys and plains, from which in the course of generations they were gradually cleared by the hand of man. The woods remained on the hills which, while not ideally suited to them, were at least safer from the depredations of man. Thus, when we speak of woodland in Israel today, we invariably think of wooded growth on the rocky hillsides.

In the last generation we witnessed the final destruction of the forests. The trees growing nearest to human habitation were the first to go, and then the more distant ones, until finally only the uninhabited areas remained wooded. The woodsmen chopped down the trees which could be used for building or as fuel, and left standing only those varieties which were useless to them. Other parts of the forest served as raw material for the charcoal burners, while lively animals reached the young growth and devoured it, so that over-grazing dealt the final blow.

'The Comb', *landmark of pine trees on a hilltop west of Jerusalem, remnant of the ancient pine forest which once clothed the hills around.*

It may seem strange that a description of the forest should begin with an account of its destruction, but it is clear that this is what happened. The whole history of the woodland is one of a struggle for survival against the encroachments of man and his implements. The species of trees which made up each forest, and the particular history of each area, led to the emergence of three basic formations:

1) *The open forest or park*: In woodland of this type the trees have a distinct central trunk and a broad expanse of foliage, and each tree is spaced well apart from its neighbour. The tree most often found in forests of this type is the Mount Tabor oak.

2) *Maquis, or macchia*: This is a common formation throughout the Mediterranean basin. The trees are not tall, rarely exceeding a height of fifteen or twenty feet, but grow quite closely together. Frequently a tree, bushlike, will have more than one trunk, and the thicket formed by such trees, bushes and creepers is often impassable.

A deep canyon in Galilee, the finest in northern Israel, Nahal Amud is a nature reserve where wild life and beautiful scenery combine.

3) *Garique*: This may be either maquis growth in the last stages of decline, or woodland just beginning to grow up again. The trees will either have been burnt or gnawed down, or may just be recovering from similar ravages. They look like bushes seven to ten feet high, with a thick undergrowth. The garique can also degenerate into heathland. The forest then is totally destroyed, leaving only unrecognizable traces of its existence.

The maquis in its various stages constitutes the principal forest growth in Israel, both in terms of acreage and in variety of species, and we shall therefore consider this first.

The general appearance of the maquis suggests that it is made up mostly of evergreens, and such deciduous species as there are do little to change this general picture. Most of the trees and bushes have hard leaves, some of them with small prickles, and quite a number of them sprout large thorns of different kinds.

As we mentioned earlier, this kind of vegetation is common to all the Mediterranean lands, though it is not exclusive to them. In regions of the same general latitude, whether north or south of the equator, with more or less the same climate and winter rains, such vegetation is typical. Some parts of California, Chile and South Africa, and certain parts of Australia, all have maquis similar to that in Israel, though with several important differences. Whereas in the Mediterranean countries the maquis is made up of identical or similar species of plants, in other regions its composition has great diversity.

The main components of the maquis in Israel include some twenty species of tree, but only two give this growth its characteristic quality. One is an evergreen oak tree, the common tree oak (*Quercus calliprinos*), and the other is the terebinth (*Pistacia palaestina*).

The botanists have never been able to decide whether the Palestine oak is a tree which came to resemble a bush under the difficult conditions of the maquis, or whether it is a bush which under special circumstances assumes the characteristics of a tree. There is much to be said for both views. In certain places, near the graves of holy men for example, several ancient massive specimens of this oak may be found. These are indisputably trees, with a single thick trunk crowned by rich foliage. On the other hand, most of the oaks of the maquis look more like bushes and, while they may be several yards high, they have several slender trunks. It is not for us to attempt to settle the argument; we can simply note that the two forms exist.

As for the terebinth, which in the maquis also grows like a large bush, it is far easier to state emphatically that it is by nature a tree. While many of the sacred terebinths with which we are familiar are of the Atlantic variety, the Palestine terebinth also appears as a large tree with a single sturdy trunk. This is the tree in which Absalom, David's son, caught his head when fleeing from the field of Ephraim and in which he met his death. The Authorized Version of the Bible refers to an oak, but in the original Hebrew the tree is described as an *elah*, terebinth.

'For the battle was there scattered over the face of the country: and the wood devoured more people that day than the sword devoured. And Absalom met the servants of David. And Absalom rode upon a mule, and the mule went under the thick boughs of a great oak, and his head caught hold of the oak, and he was taken up between the heaven and the earth; and the mule that was under him went away.' (II SAMUEL 18: 8–9)

The oak and the terebinth are not only the mainstays of the maquis, but also give it its general colouring. Here it is suitable perhaps to take a look at the colours of the maquis and to pass on to a glance at some of the other species to be found there. The other varieties are not equally distributed, but grow in lesser or greater numbers depending on the direction of the slope, the amount of moisture, and other factors.

One of the handsomest trees of the maquis is the arbutus (*Arbutus andrachne*). At first glance it seems ill-suited to its surroundings; its shiny reddish-brown trunk, its large leaves, its hanging clusters of creamy-coloured bell-like flowers and its abundant cherry-red berries appear out of place in the harsh setting of the maquis. Despite its beauty, the tree has a bad name; the reddish tint of its trunk apparently gave rise to a legend linking the tree to the story of a son who, having murdered his father, was punished by being converted into a tree carrying the signs of his sin. The arbutus occurs in the maquis in many areas, but is most common in Galilee and the Jerusalem hills.

The laurel or bay (*Laurus nobitis*) needs no introduction: its leaves made the wreath with which the victor was crowned during the Greek era, while in our own

The arbutus differs from most forest trees, with its large glossy leaves, its smooth red-brown trunk and branches, and its creamy-coloured flowers and red berries.

right: A green lizard caught in a forest clearing. It lives among trees and shrubs and has survived by perfect adaptation to its natural background.

The fragrant white blossom of the wild pear can never be hidden, even when the trees are concealed amongst the thickets of Galilee. In summer the delicious fruits provide a banquet for shepherds and for the wild life of the woodlands.

right: *A young eagle-owl, two days old, hatched in a cave in the forest; the chick will become one of the biggest of all the owls.*

left: *A field of lupins at the foot of Mount Tabor in Lower Galilee, where the hosts of Israel gathered under the Judges, Deborah and Barak, and by Christian tradition the Mount of the Transfiguration.*

Trees blown by the sea winds, on hills not far from the coast, develop this banner formation with all the growth on the leeward side.

time they are used to flavour pickles and stews. Several yards high, the laurel favours damp places in the maquis, flourishing in ravines or near water. Two trees usually found in close proximity to the laurel, especially along the banks of streams in Upper Galilee, are the maple (*Acer obtusifolium*) and the plane tree (*Platanus orientalis*). The latter is one of the largest trees in the country, both in height and in the circumference of its trunk. Its only weakness, if the term may be used, is its dependence upon the proximity of running water. With the spread of civilization, several of the streams favoured by the plane tree have either dried up or been diverted, and the trees have withered away. Nevertheless, a number still remain to lend majesty to the maquis of Galilee.

Among the flowering trees whose colours catch the eye are the styrax (*Styrax officinalis*) and the Judas tree. The former is in fact a large bush, recognizable from a distance by its distinctive foliage: the backs of its leaves are white. In the spring it puts forth an abundance of white, sweet-smelling blossoms much favoured by insects. The ancients believed in its medicinal power; hence its second name, *officionalis*. The Judas tree (*Cercis siliquastrum*) lies hidden in the maquis for the best part of the year, shedding its leaves in winter; but in the spring it bursts into bloom with pinkish papillionate flowers, which emerge straight from the thicker boughs

as well as from the smaller branches, and at this time of year it can be recognized from afar by the pinkish glow of its blossom. Its name in Hebrew means 'crown of the maquis', and in Arabic, 'bride of the maquis'. Popular legend follows strange paths: Christian tradition attributes to this tree the doubtful honour of having been chosen by Judas Iscariot for his suicide by hanging; hence its name.

While we are thinking of flowering trees, we must not forget the rose family, which makes a greater contribution than any other. Several varieties are to be found in the maquis, all distinctive for their blossom and for one other important characteristic: they all bear edible fruit — something which we have not found so far in any other tree mentioned. One of them, the wild pear (*Pyrus communis*), may be found in Galilee and on the Carmel range. The wild plum (*Prunus*), which is rarer, exists only in the uplands of Galilee. Varieties of their less fastidious cousin, the hawthorn, may be found as far afield as the steppe and even in the Negev mountains, but the best fruit comes from the Galilee hawthorn or Mediterranean medlar (*Crataegus azardolus*), and is a delicacy even for those who ordinarily scorn wild fruits. There are two varieties, yellow and red, and each has its own devotees, but both provide rich and fragrant blossoms in the spring.

Trees, most of which we have no space to describe in detail, form only one layer of the maquis; there is another above them, and sometimes one or two more below. The upper layer is composed of some ten species of creeper. Their roots are deeply embedded in the soil, their tendrils wind up the trunks of their hosts toward the light. They appear to be the sturdiest of all the vegetation in the maquis: even after all the trees have been cut down and the bushes uprooted, they continue to sprout from crevices in the rocks. We will mention only the honeysuckle (*Lonicera*), with its cream and pink flowers, two varieties of virgin's bower (*Clematis cirrhosa*) and the asparagus (*Asparagus*).

The next layer below the trees is formed by bushes and undergrowth, and it is difficult to decide whether some of these should rightly be regarded as degenerated trees or well-developed bushes. One such doubtful case is the arrow wood (*Viburnum tinus*). Fairly rare, it bears clusters of white flowers and purple fruit. Others, which have no trunk, quite clearly fall into the category of bushes. The most common is a yellow thorny broom (*Calycotome infesta*), a large thorny bush with yellow papillionate flowers. During the rainy season it is covered with green leaves, which it sheds in summer, but in March and April it is bedecked with brilliant yellow flowers in unusual abundance. Even more beautiful are the flowers of the broom (*Spartium*), especially in the maquis of Upper Galilee. The myrtle, though a flowering plant, is best known for its shiny green foliage. Two species of labdanum (*Cistus*) contribute their white and pink blossoms to the colour scheme of the maquis. Because the flowers somewhat resemble the wild rose, they have acquired the name 'rock roses'.

left: *A hidden spring in western Galilee forms a silent pool, still and smooth as a mirror.*

Trees are not in exclusive possession of the forest: the purple thistle joins their company and strives to grow as tall.

The ground level of the maquis is given over to grasses and flowers, both annuals and perennials. Few flowers really do well in the true maquis: most of them take advantage of the clearings, the garigue or the heathland, where they spread out in their thousands. When botany textbooks refer to three hundred per cent cover in the maquis, it is no exaggeration. Three or four layers of vegetation are quite normal.

For most of the year the maquis appears to be a uniform shade of green, but towards the end of summer and at the beginning of winter the green is broken by the colour of the berries and fruit, the turning leaves of some of the deciduous trees, and especially the reddish leaves shed by the terebinth. Then the grass grows tall and the leafless trees are swallowed up in the expanse of green. The biggest change comes in March, and for about two months there are variations in colour. The effect is sometimes not showy, but anyone sensitive to colour sees infinite changes and shades of changes. The year-round green is varied by the distinctive, fresher hues of leaves in bud and at every stage of their development. This is the season when even the sombre oaks relent and look a little gay, while the buds of the terebinth contribute tints ranging from reddish-purple to green. The flowering trees — both those we have mentioned and those we have passed over — add their blossoms to the symphony of colour, and it is now that the bushes really come into their own, with white, pink and yellow blooms predominating. From a distance it seems that blue is missing, but this is provided by the bottom layer, the flower level of the maquis.

right: *Even in summer, when much of the country-side is sere and yellow, the mountain slopes of western Galilee are green. Here, after the good winter rains, trees and shrubs can continue their growth through the dry season. (On the skyline, the Crusader castle of Montfort.)*

left: *Once an ugly caterpillar gorging itself on leaves, the butterfly settles for an instant on a thistle.*

Wild pink hollyhocks, growing taller than a man, mark the change from spring to summer.

Branch of Jerusalem pine (Aleppo pine), native to Israel and widely dispersed all over the northern half of the country through afforestation schemes.

Patches of maquis in the beds of wadis with either springs or a trickle of running water have a character all their own. Apart from the fact that the water-loving plants play a greater role in the overall picture — especially the plane trees — the combination of plant life, rocks and water creates a uniquely different landscape. A most striking bush is the oleander (*Nerium oleander*), its pink flowers filling the valleys with colour and scent.

We have gone into great detail in describing the maquis, though at the expense of other types of woodland. The carob, or black locust tree (*Ceratonia siliqua*), whose fruit is famous as St John's Bread, the pine and the Mount Tabor oak each produce their own particular kind of forest, depending upon the soil and climate, but in area they are far less important than the maquis. The Mount Tabor oak forests, with their trees of lordly size and commanding presence, are very impressive — especially in lower Galilee and on the Golan Heights, and single gigantic Mount Tabor oaks, or clumps of oaks, preserved because of the sanctity of a particular spot, provide beauty in a number of places in Israel.

We cannot conclude our description of the woodlands without mentioning the tremendous afforestation projects which have been carried out since the beginning of the Jewish resettlement in the nineteenth century. An important addition to the tree population was the eucalyptus, introduced from Australia and planted in the swamp areas as part of the draining process. This tree is now to be seen all over the country. Other projects, mostly undertaken by the Jewish National Fund, include the planting of tens of thousands of acres of forest with scores of millions of trees, mostly pine. Whole areas have been transformed from yellow and clothed with green, and the combination of man-made forests, natural forests and farmland recalls some of the consoling passages in the words of the Prophets of old.

'...therefore will I remember thee from the land of Jordan...'

(Psalms 42:6)

Oleander bushes, common on the banks of streams, are especially abundant along the upper reaches of the Jordan River, north of the Sea of Galilee.

PRIDE OF JORDAN

Mount Hermon is the highest peak within the boundaries of the Land of the Bible. The Dead Sea is the world's lowest point. Mount Hermon is 8,677 feet above sea level, the Dead Sea 1,233 feet below. For all their differences, the two extremes are joined by the River Jordan. A drop of water falling on the Hermon, whether as snow or dew, may eventually evaporate from the surface of the Dead Sea, though only after following a long and meandering course.

The whole distance, from the tallest peak to the southernmost tip of the Dead Sea, is only 165 miles as the crow flies; but what changes in this short distance! At one end, the snows of yesteryear have not yet melted away before they are joined by new drifts, while at the other the heat is so intense that a total depth of half an inch of water evaporates from the surface of the Dead Sea every day. This sea is eight times as salty as ordinary sea.

Let us follow the Jordan along its entire course and see the changes that occur, at practically every step, in the landscape and in the flora and fauna. Without pretending to give a full picture or attempting to give a comprehensive account of its history, we shall start out with a short summary of the valley's geology.

The course of the Jordan was determined by one of the most far-reaching geological events which has occurred on the face of the earth; the formation of the Great Rift Valley. The process began in the Tertiary period about fifty million years ago, was at its peak in the Pleistocene epoch one million years ago, and in one way or another is continuing even at the present time. In Israel it resulted in the deep

cleft which runs from the foot of Mount Hermon, through the Dead Sea to the Gulf of Eilat (which itself is part of it). Like every depression, it filled up with water over the years. The waters of the Jordan Sea, as this early stage is called, waxed and waned with changes in the climate, finally retreating into the shapes with which we are familiar from the maps of our era: three lakes (the Hula, the Sea of Galilee and the Dead Sea) linked by the river. The Hula was drained during the 1950's and has disappeared, and only the Sea of Galilee and the Dead Sea now remain.

The Jordan basin is in the bed of this former sea, and its history lies written in the soils, rich in gypsum and marl, and in the three levels which were formed, representing the various periods of the sea's shrinking. Sheer cliffs tower to heights of 4,600 feet to the east and to the west of the basin. The hills to the east, the heights of Golan and Gilead, have abundant rainfall, and can even support forest growths. The western face, descending from the hills of Samaria and Judea, forms a barrier, which stops the rains penetrating into the basin proper. Thus this slope, exposed to the sun in the east, is fairly barren, becoming more and more parched as we descend further south. From the Beth Shean Valley southwards the Jordan Valley is a narrow strip of green cutting through a barren wilderness.

Mount Hermon, source of the Jordan, and consisting mainly of hard limestone from the Jurassic period, about 150 million years ago, towers above its surroundings, and the more recent layers at the summit have been eroded away, exposing a massive peak of ancient bedrock jutting high above all the lesser peaks. Precipitation on the mountain is heavy, up to about seventy-two inches a year. More important, this precipitation does not fall as heavy rains but as snow, which gradually melts and seeps down into the porous heart of the mountain. The water does not remain there, of course, but bubbles out at the foot of the mountain in three main springs which, together with several minor streams, combine to form the headwaters of the Jordan.

On the western slope of Mount Hermon, a heavy forest growth of oak and wild fruit trees reaches right up to the timber line — about 4,600 feet. The Syrian squirrel and the snow vole, which are not to be found anywhere else in Israel, are among the inhabitants, not to mention some of the other woodland animals with which we are familiar in different parts of the country. Above the timber line the vegetation becomes thinner and more dwarfed, seeking shelter from the winds in crevices in the chalky rock. The trees become stunted and bushlike, enabling them to stand up against the gales that sweep the heights. At about 5,600 feet the uplands are covered with round balls of prickly thrift (*Acantholimon*) and the milk vetch (*Astragalus*) so common at such altitudes. We also find various species of desert birds, taking advantage of the abundance of insects. Depending on altitude, the ground is covered with snow for varying periods of the year.

The Jordan River, a capricious mountain stream between the heights of Golan and Galilee, broadens and becomes calmer as it flows through the plain, spreading into a delta before entering Lake Kinneret — the Sea of Galilee.

The little streams near the crest of the mountain give no idea of the flow at the foot. The sight of gushing water is rare enough in Israel, and only at the foot of Mount Hermon can it be seen in several places at once. The largest of the three principal tributaries of the Jordan, the Dan, is also the shortest. It has its source in the little nature reserve next to Tel Dan, its broad flow dividing into several streams once it reaches level ground. At this point, it waters one of the best known woods in the country, the Tal Grove, with its great ancient oaks, some of them hundreds of years old. They are all that remain of the forests which probably covered the area in ancient times. When all the other woodlands were cleared, these were spared, thanks to the supernatural powers with which the Moslem inhabitants of Upper Galilee believed them to be endowed.

The Banias, or Nahal Hermon, is the tributary with the most beautiful valley. It bursts forth from the living rock at the foot of Mount Hermon, next to the cave which served the Canaanites and the Greeks alike as a place of worship — the name 'Banias' is a corruption of 'Pan', god of the shepherds. As it continues on its way, it cuts a deep bed through a dense woodland of trees and flowering oleander. Its banks are lined with blackberry bushes whose lush dark fruits are the best in the country.

The Hatzbani, or Nahal Snir, although the longest of the tributaries, is not very different from the others; like them it has clumps of willows along its banks.

A smaller stream, Nahal Ijon, which does not rise on Mount Hermon, gives the nature reserve its four waterfalls — something not to be seen again along the Jordan basin until Ein Gedi. Its waters only flow for six months of the year. In March and April two of the falls, the 'Mill' and the 'Oven', together provide the biggest attraction for hikers in this part of the country and, from June onwards, the waters are used to irrigate the lands of the Ijon Valley. The plants to be found here are not unusual, but their associations are uncommon; flowers native to the woodlands of Galilee, such as the snapdragon (*Antirrhinum*) and the bell flower (*Michauxia*), are to be found growing next to common water plants. Lining the river banks are clusters of pink oleander and the blue blossoms of the chaste tree (*Vitex agnus-castus*). Nature lovers come to the 'Oven' in spring to catch a glimpse of a

The young fry of the tilapia have a safe refuge in the mouth of their parent when danger threatens in the waters of Lake Kinneret.

Great white herons, honoured guests in winter in the Jordan Valley, come to visit the fish-ponds.

left: *The Dead Sea sparrow lives only in the Jordan Valley. It builds a nest of rough twigs disproportionate in size to such a tiny bird. Weighing three pounds or so, it can be used year after year, needing only minor repairs.*

The Hula nature reserve retains in miniature the character of the original lake and swamp, now largely drained to make way for fields and fishponds. The papyrus (right) provides a nesting place for water birds while the yellow-bloomed Jus-siaea (left), floating on its air-filled roots, 'walks' across the water.

very rare bird, the wall creeper (*Tichodroma muraria*), which can occasionally be seen in a crevice in the cliff as it flutters its great red and black wings. This sight repays all the trouble of getting there.

The tributaries join to form the river, but only for a short distance. In the past, the Jordan split after a few miles into two main streams which in turn lost themselves in the great fen of the Hula. The swamp has been drained for more than a decade, as well as the lake to the south, and only a small nature reserve is left to recall its verdant past, but the Hula region was a wonder of nature worthy to be described in detail here.

Lake Hula, with an area of 3,750 acres, and the swamp to the north of it, three times this size, together formed a single entity. The Jordan River and several minor streams flowed into it from the north, east and west, and the outflow at the southern end ran into the Sea of Galilee. The water was shallow and still, with a maximum depth of eighteen feet in the lake, and never exceeded six feet in the swamp. This abundance of water combined with organic material which had collected there in the course of centuries to nourish a lush and heavy vegetation, which spread out from the shores of the lake and extended to the dry land all round. Six zones of plant life could be clearly identified around the lake, according to the depth of water.

The most striking flowers in the lake, the water lilies, set the water scene, while tall clumps of papyrus (*Cyperus papyrus*) waved above the marshlands. The papyrus, which still reigns supreme in the Hula nature reserve, is known throughout Africa.

140

A true tropical plant, it has accompanied the material and intellectual progress of civilization through thousands of years. It was used in the weaving of reed mats, and for the walls of primitive huts and most important, in making the first paper for writing. The word paper in itself bears testimony to its origin. This swampland, several thousand acres in area, was the only place in Israel where the papyrus grew, and it also provided a unique habitat for a thriving wild life of its own.

The lake and the swamp came to life at the end of winter, with the first warm breezes. All the vegetation would burst into bloom at once — the white and orange water lilies (*Nymphaea*), the yellow flags, and a wealth of other flowers in white, yellow and violet. The animal life was no less rich. The water swarmed with various species of fish, from the little cyprinodont (*Aphanius*), only two inches long, to the giant catfish (*Clarius lazera*) weighing forty-five pounds. The herbivorous fish thrived upon the decaying vegetation, while the carnivorous catfish lived on the smaller fish. Snails and shellfish and water turtles shared the lake with the fish, together with a host of invertebrates filling every conceivable ecological niche, in the lake and in the swamp.

The most notorious denizen of the Hula swamp, and the creature on whose account it was drained, was the mosquito (*Anopheles*), the carrier of malaria. Travellers in the last century used both pen and brush to depict the unfortunate inhabitants of the Hula Valley, dwelling in rush huts, raising water buffaloes for a living and infected by incurable malaria. The children who survived infancy had

Still life, by the greatest artist: in the waters of the Dead Sea nothing lives, but trees grew around it when the level was lower than now.

Their picturesque remains, encrusted with salt crystals, contribute to an awesome landscape.

A female francolin, with sober brown and grey plumage. The male is a beautiful sight, flashing black and white in the meadows of the Beth Shean Valley.

swollen bellies resulting from their overgrown spleens, this being the organ charged with fighting the battle against the dread disease. The Jewish settlements which were established in the region, beginning in the last quarter of the 19th century, suffered from malarial fever as well, paying a high price in lives for their daring, but in contrast to the original inhabitants, who accepted malaria as the will of God, these Jewish farmers took steps to stamp it out, and they succeeded. During the 1950's, as the drainage of the lake and the swamps proceeded, the public health authorities scored a total victory: not a single new case of malaria was recorded.

The crowning glory of the Hula region was its bird life. The course of the Jordan had long been an attraction for migratory birds, both as a landmark and as a source of food on a journey which took them over long stretches of desert, and if the Jordan was an attraction. the Hula was an even greater one. Here, the water was just the right depth for any water fowl, while food was abundant and the place was safe. From the beginning of the autumn migrations up to the end of the nesting season — in fact for most of the year — the Hula was the scene of constantly changing bird life, in their comings and goings, in the air and on the water, fishing or feeding their voracious young.

During the winter the lake and swamp pools were dotted with coots and wild ducks, and at least two species of wild duck nested there in summer. The coots did not breed in the Hula region though their relatives, the moorhens (*Gallinula chloropus*), raised their tiny long-toed chicks, like balls of black fluff, beside the lake and the young used to walk on the broad leaves of the water lilies. In sharp contrast to the black plumage of the moorhens was the white of the pelicans (*Pelecanus onocrotalus*), which would come down for fish, hundreds at a time, a line of fishing pelicans moving across the water and driving the fish before them. When the fish concentration was high enough they would thrust their pouched beaks below the surface, coming up with giant mouthfuls of water and fish. With water streaming from the sides of their beaks they gulped the fish down into their insatiable stomachs.

Studies show that a hungry pelican can devour as much as thirteen pounds of fish in a day.

But the Hula has been drained and, where once there were marshes and lake, cotton fields and fishponds now flourish. A small area, some 750 acres in all, has been left as a nature reserve, with its characteristic swamps and waterways remaining. There is even a herd of water buffaloes (*Bubalus bubalis*) wallowing there, just as they used to do in the past, though it is difficult to include in such a small area everything that was once to be found in the region. The birds, for example, have not accepted the fishponds as substitutes for the shallow lake, while the fish seem to have lost some of their favourite grounds and are no longer so numerous, and the wild boars have no place to roam, trapped between the fields and the ponds. That is the price for the march of civilization.

South of the Hula the Jordan enters a narrow defile between two slopes of basalt rock, and its course drops 860 feet in the next ten miles. Because of the steepness of its banks the river here leaves little mark on the surrounding countryside, and it becomes a narrow stream, splashing out into the open now and then between thick clumps of oleander and black, water-smoothed rocks. Along the slopes are wild Christ-thorn (*Zizyphus*), their delicious fruit a feast for shepherds and jackals alike.

After this steep descent the Jordan disappears for a while into Lake Kinneret. The lake — or Sea of Galilee — is a gem set into the surrounding landscape. For the layman it is not particularly rich in plant or animal life, although the biologist finds abundant material for study. The land around the lake has been cultivated for thousands of years, and most of the natural growth has long since vanished.

Anyone acquainted with the New Testament must associate the Sea of Galilee with fish and fishermen; the first of the Apostles were called from its shores and from this trade: 'And Jesus, walking by the Sea of Galilee, saw two brethren, Simon called Peter, and Andrew his brother, casting a net into the sea: for they were fishers. And he saith unto them, Follow me, and I will make you fishers of men. And they straightway left their nets, and followed him. And going on from thence, he saw other two brethren, James the son of Zebedee, and John his brother, in a ship with Zebedee their father, mending their nets; and he called them. And they immediately left the ship and their father, and followed him.' (Matthew 4: 18–22).

Not less memorable is the miracle of the loaves and fishes: 'And when it was evening, his disciples came to him, saying, This is a desert place, and the time is now past; send the multitude away, that they may go into the villages, and buy themselves victuals. But Jesus said unto them, They need not depart; give ye them to eat. And they say unto him, We have here but five loaves and two fishes. He said, Bring them hither to me. And he commanded the multitude to sit down on the grass, and took the five loaves, and the two fishes, and looking up to heaven, he blessed, and brake,

above: *Water lilies, half-hidden by their glossy green leaves, surprise the visitor to the Hula nature reserve in June, not least by the contrast between their dazzling beauty and the muddy swamps around.*

overleaf right above: *Mount Hermon is snow-clad for many months of the year, but by the end of summer snow has yielded to sun, and small patches only remain to greet fresh falls.*

overleaf: *Waterfall on the Banias, Nahal Hermon, one of the three main tributaries which join to form the Jordan River. Perhaps the largest in Israel, it is divided by an ancient plantain, defying the force of the waters.*

overleaf right below: *The blue waters of the Sea of Galilee, Lake Kinneret, calm in summer, will rage with man-high waves in the tempests of winter.*

and gave the loaves to his disciples, and the disciples to the multitude. And they did all eat, and were filled: and they took up of the fragments that remained twelve baskets full. And they that had eaten were about five thousand men, beside women and children.' (Matthew 14: 15–21).

The scientific names of some of the fish in this lake contain references to the Galilee of Roman times, or to early Christianity, such as the Galilee cyclid (*Tilapia galilea*), *Tristramella sacra* and *Tristramella simonis*, the last two discovered by the British zoologist Tristram in Lake Kinneret in the last century. There is also a small fish called *Haplochronis josepii flavii*, after the well-known Jewish historian of the 1st century AD. Up to our own time, the waters of the lake abound with fish, amongst them some unique to the Jordan basin, such as the species of *Tilapia* (St Peter's Fish). Some of the *Tilapia* have a very special way of hatching and rearing their young, carrying their eggs, and later the young fry, about in their mouths. Even after the fry begin to swim and forage for themselves, the parent's mouth still serves as a refuge to which they can flee in time of trouble.

Outstanding among the fowl that frequent the lake is the great crested grebe (*Podiceps cristatus*) with its elegant plumage, which lays its eggs and makes its home along the water's edge. Since they swim quite close in to the shore, they form a very decorative part of the scenery, for travellers on the road that rings the lake. They share the landscape with the gulls, particularly the lesser black-backed gull and the herring gull. Another inhabitant of the shores of the Sea of Galilee, the blind fresh–water shrimp, will be considered in the chapter on invertebrates.

From the Sea of Galilee to the Dead Sea the Jordan follows a winding course which nearly trebles the distance as our crow would fly. There are places where it runs swift and deep, and others where its flow is broad and sluggish, leaving behind small islands and peninsulas. As we move still further south, closer to the fringes of the desert, nothing can survive unless it has direct contact with water. The Jewish farmers take their banana plantations and cotton fields down as close as they can to the bank of the river, and the whole stretch from the lake southwards to the Beth Shean Valley is a vast patchwork of cultivated fields, settlements and fishponds, which do not allow the river to develop vegetation of its own. Even so, bottom land growth begins to appear; the 'swelling' or 'pride of Jordan' mentioned in Jeremiah 12: 5 and 49: 19 and Zechariah 11: 3. But it is only further south, where the Jordan emerges from the settled areas and reaches near-wilderness, that the 'swelling' comes into its own. Here it becomes a real forest, consisting mainly of tamarisk, willow and poplar trees, crowding together along the banks and widening out to fill the bends in the river. The bigger trees, hung with creepers climbing up out of a rich undergrowth, sometimes form an impassable thicket. In biblical times, this jungle-like growth was frequented by beasts of prey — bears and lions — and it is probably thanks to them that the prophets adopted the phrase 'pride of Jordan', signifying both beauty and awe. The two she-bears mentioned in the story of Elisha in II Kings 2:24 emerged from the forest along the way from Jericho to Beth-el. While the location may have been in the hills, it might just as well have been in this very 'pride of Jordan'.

Today, nothing more dangerous is left than the jungle cat, of whom more will be said later: driven by the draining of its natural swampland habitat, it thrives near the artificial fishponds of the farming settlements round about. Native otters and mongoose have also benefited from the ponds, as has a more recent immigrant, the coypu (*Myocaster coypus*). The latter were first imported from South America to be bred for their fur. While few have been turned into fur coats, the ones that escaped have succeeded in making themselves very much at home in and around the fishponds.

The thicket is a paradise for birds. The storks follow the Jordan basin in their spring migrations, and it is a thrilling sight to see a flock perched for the night on the trees, like so many great white flowers. Far noisier are the twilight assemblies of vast flocks of starlings. They begin to gather about an hour before sunset, some of them from miles away, descending in black, chattering clouds on the Jordan thicket. It takes them an hour or more to get ready for sleep, flitting in and out of the wood and hopping from branch to branch until they find one to their liking. The coming of darkness finally brings the tumult to an end.

In the quiet backwaters of the river, on inaccessible dead tree trunks, colonies of herons and egrets can be found; the squacco heron (*Ardeola ralloides*) and night heron (*Nycticorax nycticorax*), cattle egret (*Ardeola ibis*) and little egret (*Egretta garzetta*). There may be as many as 300 nests, representing three or four species, in a single colony. It would be hard to imagine a more vivid and lively scene than a community of herons in which every stage of the life cycle, from courting through birth to death is taking place before your eyes.

Also worth mentioning are the Dead Sea sparrows (*Passer moabiticus*), little birds of which two sub-species exist, each inhabiting a different area. One lives in the Jordan Valley and the Tigris-Euphrates basin, and the other in central Asia.

As the Jordan draws closer to the Dead Sea, draining the land it passes through, its flow becomes ever stronger, and its surroundings more and more desert-like. The last reaches of the river, before its waters enter the Dead Sea, are perhaps the most famous in history. Here Joshua crossed the Jordan, and made his first camping place in the land of Canaan. Here are the plains of Jericho, where poor King Zedekiah was captured by the Chaldees while trying to escape from his lost kingdom. Here, too, is the traditional place of the baptism of Jesus by St John the Baptist; and so one could go on, recounting events which were enacted in the small area round about.

The River Dan, shortest but most abundant among the sources of the Jordan, where Jeroboam set up his golden calf.

*The River Jordan at the point where
it emerges from the Sea of Galilee,
to flow southwards to the Dead Sea.*

Until the changes of recent decades, there was nothing to disturb the river in the last few miles of its course. Its waters flowed through a desert of marl and salt, between banks lined on both sides with reeds, tamarisk and willows, spreading in the last mile into a delta, before losing themselves in the Dead Sea.

The admirers of this 'sea' object to its name, and say that it is full of interest, but even they cannot deny that its waters are completely devoid of life. A mosaic map of the sixth century, discovered in Jordan (the Medaba mosaic), conveys this fact most artistically: at the end of the Jordan two fish are seen, one swimming towards the Dead Sea, meeting the other on the way back, as if to say, 'It's no place for fish!' This is not surprising, as the waters of the lake contain a very high concentration of various mineral salts, which no creature can tolerate.

The Dead Sea is an insatiable maw; every day of the year half an inch of water is evaporated over the 300 square miles of its surface. The water which flows into it from the Jordan River and other streams would be enough to raise its level by fifteen feet every year, but all is turned to vapour by the scorching sun, which keeps it at a constant level — about 1,200 feet below sea level, the lowest point on earth.

Yet the Dead Sea is a real pearl of the desert of Judea. What it lacks in fauna and flora, it makes up for in the constantly changing colours of the sea itself and the high mountains surrounding it. Indeed, there is so much variation in colours that one might perhaps claim to have seen there the whole range of the spectrum. There are terribly hot and hazy days, when hardly anything is visible — and crystal-clear days, when every single crevice shows sharp contours on the farthest mountains, and it is possible to see clearly as far as seventy miles away. The most wonderful colours and startling changes are at sunrise and at sunset.

Such is the Jordan River, flowing, in its course of less than 200 miles, from the high alpine terrain of Mount Hermon to the depths of the scorching desert.

'I am the rose of Sharon, and the lily of the valleys.'

(Song of Solomon 2:1)

Wild chrysanthemums are generally observed in their myriads, carpeting whole areas, but the single blooms are no less attractive.

THE ROSE AND THE LILY

Only two flowers appear by name in the whole of the Old Testament: the rose and the lily. And even of these two, no one can say for sure to which botanical species they belong. Must it then be supposed that in those days there were no other flowers in the country or, alternatively, that our forefathers were not sufficiently aware of them to mention them? Probably neither. Hundreds of species of attractive wild flowers are to be found in Israel, and there is no doubt that they were already here long before the Bible was written. With the same degree of assurance we can say that the early Hebrews were extremely perceptive and observant and that they were certainly familiar with the flowers of the countryside. Quite simply, the Bible was not intended as a textbook on natural history and the plants which appear in it are mentioned solely to illustrate the ideas which are being expounded. It is not surprising that the only two flowers mentioned appear in the Song of Solomon, a book in which the natural beauties of this countryside figure in equal prominence with the lovers.

Israel is rich in flowers. Going out into the fields in March and April one is overwhelmed by the vigour of the season and the abundance of varieties, shapes and colours. This is especially true for anyone whose previous visits to the country have been during the dry season, between June and September, when most of the uncultivated land has turned yellow and dry. This too is another characteristic of plant life in Israel: its concentration into one season of the year.

About 2,800 species of flowering plants have been recorded in Israel. Scores of these are trees and bushes, several hundred are true grasses and many hundreds more

The Nazareth iris, grow
ing near there and els
where in Galilee and th
Golan Heights, but in n
other place in the worl

The yellow flag blooms in swamps in spring. Throughout the northern hemisphere, it thrives wherever it finds water.

fall into the category of grasses because their flowers are so minute that they fail to attract attention. After substracting all these, there remain a few hundreds (no one can say exactly how many, as it depends on personal feelings) of 'flowers' in the ordinary sense of the term. Some of them are to be found in unbelievable abundance, while others are so rare as to border on extinction.

We feel obliged from time to time to remind the reader that Israel lies at the meeting place of different geographical regions. At the risk of repeating ourselves, we feel that this point must be fully understood in order to appreciate how such an abundant variety of plant life came to exist here. Within the space of one hour it is possible to walk from a Mediterranean landscape, through inland steppe, and right to the edge of the desert, so that it is not surprising that one side of a hill has vegetation entirely different from the other. The wide range of climates and sub-climates gives each plant an opportunity to find the spot most ideally suited to its needs.

Most plants follow the same cycle. They germinate between October and December, when the soil is sure to be moist; blossom in the warm sunlight of March and April, when the air buzzes with insect life; mature and go to seed in May, and die, or at least become dormant, during the arid months between May and September, when not a drop of water is to be had. This is the recipe for survival which has been found by annuals and perennials alike.

Prominent flowers in Israel are the bulbous plants, and they can claim most of the species on which the country's fame as a flower centre rests. Many of the more celebrated cultivated flowers have relatives in the same genus growing wild in this country: the iris, tulip, lily, hyacinth, cyclamen, anemone, to name but a few. When it comes to fragrance, size and variety, some of the cultivated species outshine their more modest relatives growing wild among the rocks and hills. But size is not always the most important element in judging a flower's beauty, and some of the wild flowers are serious rivals of the cultivated species.

Summer dormancy does not harm a bulb. On the contrary, while the topsoil is covered with its dry, dead leaves, very important changes are taking place in the bulb lying beneath the surface. The first glimpse of these changes comes during the summer itself, before the first drop of rain has fallen.

All along the seashore, large white flowers shoot up out of the sands. They belong to the sea daffodil (*Pancratium maritimum*). Some scholars identify them with the 'rose of Sharon' of the Song of Solomon, while others say they are none other than the 'lilies of the field' (*krinon*) referred to by St Matthew: 'And why take ye thought for raiment? Consider the lilies of the field, how they grow, they toil not, neither do they spin: And yet I say unto you, that even Solomon in all his glory was not arrayed like one of these.' (St Matthew 6: 28–29). Blossoming as they do during the dry season, they make a greater impression than they would if they flowered while all around was lush and green.

The 'rose of Sharon' is still in full blossom when the stalks of the sea squill (*Urginea maritima*), a yard or more high, begin to appear, their entire length studded with buds. They grow all over the country, even in the most barren places, springing straight up out of completely arid soil which had given no hint of their presence. Only if you dig beneath the shoot will you come upon the enormous bulb, which stores up nourishment for years so that, when the end of summer comes, it can send up this giant spike of blooms. The stalks stand for about a month, filling the landscape with what look like tall white candles. Their season coincides with the Hebrew month of Elul, the eve of the Jewish High Holidays, when the orthodox traditionally go to visit the graves of their loved ones and the tall squills join them in symbolic tribute.

There are other bulbous plants which blossom before the rains, and they probably have good reason; the competition for the attention of insects is less, making fertilization more certain. We cannot list them all here, but one modest yet beautiful bloom deserves special mention: the Spafford *Sternbergia*. This rare orange flower, native to Israel, was first found in Galilee and the Jerusalem hills, but in recent years has also made its appearance in the highlands of the Negev. It has no stem, but blossoms on the ground, a habit which in no way detracts from its beauty and charm. The *Sternbergia* is followed by crocus (*Crocus*) and autumn crocus (*Colchicum*). While in Europe these flowers mark the end of winter and the beginning of spring, in Israel their white, pink and pale mauve blooms herald the end of summer and the beginning of the rainy season.

In the wake of the first drops of rain in October-November, the country is covered with a green carpet which lasts until it is scorched up by the east wind, announcing the return of summer in April-May. The first wave of autumn flowers is followed by a slack period. The winter brings not only life-giving water but also the cold

...mmer is in full swing, ...e earth dry and cracked, ...t the molucella blooms ...hindered, sheltering its ...all white flowers in big ...mpet-like calyxes.

Totter grass: though not flowers in the ordinary meaning of the term, botanically they can compare with any.

temperatures which slow down plant activity for a month of two, though the period is shorter in the desert and longer in the hills of Galilee. Three flowers defy the chill winds to reign unchallenged over the entire landscape, their bulbs and corms ignoring the vagaries of the climate and going ahead with their development in accordance with their inner promptings. These three are the narcissus, the cyclamen and the anemone.

The narcissus (*Narcissus*) is generally the only spot of colour to be seen in the otherwise monotonous winter landscape of the swamplands. Seeing the white petals with the orange crown in the centre, it is easy to understand how, more than 2,500 years ago, the Greeks came to compose the legend of Narcissus to explain the growth of this beautiful flower in the heart of the swamp.

The cyclamens (*Cyclamen*), spread their decorative heart-shaped leaves among the rocks, and from their midst spring the single, crown-like, long-stemmed blooms. In contrast to most other wild flowers in Israel, which bloom only for very short periods, the cyclamen goes to the other extreme: the first blossoms can be seen in November, and even sometimes in October, while the last ones remain in flower, in Upper Galilee, till May.

The anemones (*Anemone*) contribute a new dimension of colour to the landscape. Except for yellow, they come in every shade; white, pink, red, blue and purple. It is not by mere chance that they are the flowers most sought after for picking, and they suffer accordingly. Whereas the cyclamens have broad flat corms, anemones have such tiny ones that you wonder how they can nourish such abundant flowers. They can be found everywhere from the Negev to Galilee. Later in the winter, when the red anemone reigns supreme, whole fields appear to be ablaze with their blooms. Then, the connoisseurs can be found in isolated spots, searching for the purple and white varieties.

The bright, warm days of February start the great rebirth of the annuals. They have taken advantage of the first part of the winter to germinate and take root, and now they burst out of the ground and grow at a rate that can literally be measured from day to day. They jostle over every bit of soil and ray of light, and compete for the favours of every insect. The loser will perish without descendants and every

160

The white michaux-
ia, carrying flowers
of an unusual shape
on tall branching
stems, shines out
against the green
of the forest.

resource is mobilized for the struggle, not least the power to adapt, which has been acquired in the course of millions of years of independent survival and co-existence with the insect world.

They grow in every conceivable niche and cranny, in cracks in the rocks and in windswept deserts, one on top of the other with yet a third in their shade. The flowers employ all sorts of strategies to attract insects, with a variety of colours, shapes and fragrances. There are species of arum, for example, which are interested in attracting insects that thrive on compost and dead vegetation. To gain the attention of its prospective insect visitors this plant (*Arum palaestinum*), with its peculiar blossom, provides them with their favourite smell. (Needless to say, they do not smell so sweet to human noses.) Where one flower cannot be depended on a hundred are sent forth, so that at least one will be fertilized and go to seed, to ensure the coming of the next generation.

During February the first of the great irises, a perfectly delightful group of flowers unique to Israel, begin to appear in the hills round Nazareth and in the northern

left: *Few flowers can compete with the pheasant's eye narcissus in colour, scent and popularity. In Israel they are amongst the first to bloom in winter on the mountains and in the marshlands, where they look equally beautiful against the rocks or among the rich dark colourings of the swmpa.*

The white Pancratium maritimum, *sea daffodil, springs from the sand among rocks along the Mediterranean shore in the dry summer months.*

above: *The cyclamen, white or pink, flowers in the mountains of the Mediterranean zone throughout the winter, the blooms, like coronets, competing with its heart-shaped leaves in natural beauty.*

The anemone reigns as queen of all the flowers in Israel, blooming over hill and dale in red, white, cream or purple for five months of the year.

right: *Helleborine, one of the thirty members of the orchid family, whose exotic blooms are to be found from the high mountains of the north to the ravines of the Judean Desert.*

The wild artichoke, with its cruel prickles, raises its head of showy purple.

below: *The wild tulip of Israel, deep red in colour, cannot compete with its cultivated relatives in range of hues, though in beauty of form it is their equal.*

...e sea squill signals
...e changing seasons
...September.

...t: Yellow chrysan-
...mums, with other
...mposite flowers of
...milar hue, clothe
...e land with gold in
...ring.

Negev. This group of irises (*Iris* spp.) comprises about fifteen species, all of them growing at the edge of the steppe region of the Middle East. Nobody can say their exact number because they vary very much, and what one botanist regards as a single species may be divided by his colleagues into several. Anyway, at least eight species, i.e. half the total number known in the world, are native to Israel. Let us mention some of them:

The Nazareth iris grows chiefly in the hills in the immediate vicinity of the city, and this explains the special significance it holds for Christians. But no flower-lover can fail to be transported by the rare sight of the flowers spilling over the hillside in a combination of hues that beggars description. It does not seem possible that such large and exquisite flowers can grow wild, withstanding all the rigours of the cold winds which blow across these hills in winter, but in fact they do. In spite of this, they have very particular requirements; each kind is found only in a certain very limited area, and it is extremely difficult to raise them elsewhere. Neither the Mediterranean zone nor the desert seem to agree with them, and they flourish only on the border between the two, in a narrow strip which is neither too dry nor too moist, neither too cold nor too hot, like a kind of horticultural Goldilocks.

These irises grow from rhizomes. Like the bulbs, they are dormant throughout the summer, coming to life in the winter, when for a short season they bloom in all their glory. The purple iris along the coast, and the Mariae iris in the northern Negev, have brilliant purple and violet flowers. On the upper reaches of Mount Gilboa, Hayne's iris is only found in an area that cannot exceed more than a few hundred acres. Its flowers are unusually large and rounded. Later on in the season Lortet's iris, in Upper Galilee, steals the show with its delicate lilac shades.

Red and blue are not particularly common among wild flowers, but when we do come across one of the relatively few species that have these colours the blossom is large and striking. We have already mentioned the anemone. Before it has quite finished blooming it hands over the reins to its relative, the scarlet buttercup, which is a much more brilliant red. The buttercup has fibrous roots, and is thus better able to withstand drought. Another flower of the same hue is the Pheasant's Eye (*Adonis palaestina*), an annual with tiny roots which is related to the buttercup and the anemone. But the prize must go to the peony (*Paeonia mascula*), with its purple tinge, which grows only on one high mountain in Israel and blooms for just two weeks in April. Its devotees have no choice but to make a pilgrimage to the spot on foot, as they do every year without fail.

Another striking red flower is the tulip (*Tulipa*), with its six petals arranged in a cup shape. Each flower has its own stem, and each stem its own bulb. In fact there are three species of tulip: the mountain tulip, the Negev tulip and the Sharon tulip, and each has its own particular shape and its individual shade of red. A relative of

The white crocus, very fragrant, is a typical winter flower in Israel.

the local tulip, apparently a native of the mountains of Persia, was the ancestor of the tulips which the Turks introduced to Europe. Its descendants have since been scattered throughout the civilized world in thousands of shapes and colours, an ornament to every garden and every flower show.

The parade of red flowers concludes with the poppy. This hardy annual blooms by the million, covering whole hills and valleys with its vivid red blossom. It can be seen well into June, long after all the other plants with red flowers have either become completely dormant or died.

Of the blue wild flowers we will recall two, the hyacinth and the lupin. Unlike its cultivated relative, which grows in many colours, the wild hyacinth (*Hyacinthus orientalis*), which in Israel is found in Galilee, flowers only in blue, with slight variations in shading. If our wild flower cannot compete with the cultivated one in colour, in scent it is more than a match, and the traveller through Galilee in March will have a fragrant journey. The lupin (*Lupinus*) spike carries a large number of papillionate flowers in a lovely violet-blue colour, tinting whole valleys, and hillsides too where the soil is heavy.

Seen from a distance, and at different times, the fields of wild flowers seem to change colour in wave after wave, as if several species of plants had come to an agreement amongst themselves as to which ones of like colour would bloom simultaneously. Thus large areas will be stained with purple, with pink or with several intermediate colours, representing the flowers of different species, each succeeding the other. The most striking example, however, is the sovereignty of yellow. The large families, containing the mustard and the composites, are represented by many species with a multitude of flowers. Their yellow blossoms, whether four-petalled or inflorescent, turn thousands of acres to brilliant gold, penetrating everywhere, spreading like wildfire over the fields, infiltrating among the stalks of grain, clambering over every ruin, climbing hillsides and spreading across the plains of the Negev. No one has yet managed to define the exact number of species, but there must be scores. While it is hard to choose one for special mention, at least the chrysanthemum (*Chrysanthemum*) should be named, if only because of

its large size and ubiquity. Like several other flowers mentioned above, the wild chrysanthemum is the ancestor of many cultivated flowers of that name which are so popular throughout the world.

March, and especially April, bring with them an unbelievable abundance of flowers. Wherever you go, you walk on multi-coloured carpets, large flowers, small flowers, and then even smaller ones, climbing one on top of the other, pushing their way into every crevice, competing for the attention of every passing insect. The climax comes quickly and is swiftly followed by the anti-climax. Some of the flowers do not even wait for the hot winds of the end of April and the beginning of May and disappear while the fields are still fresh and green; their seeds are maturing while the soil is still moist, or nourishment is stored away in their bulbs. Others only cease flowering with the first breath of the scorching east wind.

Then the landscape begins to change colour; the green gives way to tan, which spreads from the desert to the hills. The flowers fade before the advancing brown, leaving field after field, and remain only in the wooded hills and on the northern slopes of the mountains. By May, when the valleys and low hills are already thoroughly dry, the rambler on Mount Carmel or in the mountains of Galilee finds himself in an entirely different world: there the land is still green, and the flowers are still boldly blooming. In the ravines of Galilee the pink blossoms of the wild snap-dragon and the white michauxia are still to be found.

Near the mountain tops, far from man's encroachments, the madonna lily (*Lilium candidum*) grows larger and more beautiful than the garden variety. This flower has a special significance for Christians: in almost all the pictures showing the angel Gabriel appearing to the Virgin Mary, the angel carries a bunch of white lilies, the madonna lily. Perhaps the explanation of the rarity of this beautiful flower in Israel now, lies in the desire of the pilgrims of the past to pluck the flowers and their bulbs, to take home with them as a living reminder of the Annunciation, as shown in these pictures.

170

An unmistakable feature of the countryside of Israel, thistles grow everywhere in unbelievable abundance. Most belong to two families, parsley and composite. Skeletons of Atractylis (left), Gundelia (far left) *and* Scolymus (below) *fill the summer landscape.*

Brilliant red poppies succeed the fad-ing anemones and ranunculi in spring, sometimes blooming as late as June.

White and yellow 'parasols' of the parsley family cover waste lands in May, providing nectar for bees when the orange blossom fades.

Orchards and vineyards are densely carpeted in late winter with the flowers of the purple catchfly (Silene), *a small annual of prolific growth.*

On the beaches, the bindweed (*Convolvulus*) and the morning glory blossom forth in white flowers as they spread across the sands. Strangely enough, here a newcomer reigns supreme; the evening primrose (*Oenothera*), brought from America only 200 years ago, but which has made itself completely at home. Its big yellow flowers open at dusk, exposing wide areas of nectar and pollen to the ministrations of the moths.

No account of the plant life of the Bible would be complete without mentioning the thistles, which are perhaps even more characteristic of the country than its flowers. Towards the end of the winter season, a large part of the vegetation acquires that thorny appearance so widespread in arid countries. Neither the farmer nor the hiker has any use for them, regarding them only as a prickly, harmful nuisance. But if one can rise for a moment above the strictly utilitarian approach and look at them from the aesthetic point of view, it is possible to appreciate their special charms and understand why some of the richest companies in the world adorn their office waiting rooms with thistles from this country. The best are members of the composite and parsley families. Thistles of every shape — straight, bent, twisted lengthwise and across, and ranging in colour from light yellow to deep brown, punctuate the landscape and nod gaily in the breeze as they scatter their seed 'as the chaff of the mountains before the wind, and like a rolling thing before the whirlwind.' (Isaiah 17: 13).

The summer passes, the days grow shorter and a new smell is in the air. The sea squill again shoots up and out of the dry soil, and a new cycle of flowers has begun.

'...that which the locust hath left hath the canker-worm eaten; and that which the cankerworm hath left hath the caterpillar eaten.'

(Joel 1:4)

The hairy caterpillar of the Sturnia pyri *moth. The four wings of the adult have a pattern similar to an eye, one at the centre of each.*

THE MOVING CREATURE THAT HATH LIFE

There are countless species of invertebrates in Israel and any attempt to arrive at their number would be a hopeless task, especially if we include the offshore waters of the Mediterranean and the Red Sea. In a country where additional species of vertebrates are still being identified, the discovery of new invertebrates has become commonplace. Let it suffice to say that the figure runs into tens of thousands, of which the overwhelming majority are insects.

The invertebrates have not won a very savoury reputation for themselves in the sight of man. If we exclude the butterflies, which have succeeded in stirring the imagination of children and poets (and incidentally arousing the enmity of farmers, who meet these insects as caterpillars devastating their crops) and also omit the bees, whose sting we are prepared to overlook in exchange for honey, we are left with a host of wreckers, the bane of books, clothes, crops and fruits. As though this were not enough, they even try to compete with man for the sovereignty of the world. These prejudices, partly borne of experience, partly a legacy from the past and partly an error of observation and understanding, will just have to be suspended for a time, while we take a short journey through the invertebrate world of Israel.

The basic groups of invertebrates are universal, though of course the species differ from country to country. Thus we find grasshoppers and butterflies, beetles and bees, snails and spiders, worms and sea urchins. Many of these species were discovered here, or are found only in Israel, some of them being rare creatures whose names are known only to naturalists. Let us look closely at one of them, the blind fresh-water

When the first rains moisten the ground, snails which have been dormant through the summer months emerge from their holes, leaving a trail of silver behind them as they crawl along the paths and grasses.

shrimp (*Typhlocaris*), which has several extraordinary characteristics. While there are related species living in two or three other places in the world, those in Israel, numbering a few score at most, are unique of their kind and live in one spring at the northern end of the Sea of Galilee. Just between the Christian shrines of the Church of the Loaves and Fishes, the Mount of Beatitudes and Capernaum there is a group of seven springs, which the Greeks called the Heptapagon. One of them is a hot spring, whose water gushes up at a temperature of between 73° F (23° C) and 80° F (27° C). Above the spring is an interesting building, whose walls enclose the spring waters, raising them to a level which creates a waterfall, to drive a water mill. It is here, in the warm water, that the blind shrimp makes its home. In spite of all the limitations, it finds enough food, groping its way through the water to seek out its prey with its long antennae. Its transparent body is only two inches long. Experiments have shown

Amongst the snails, some are active all the year round, to the chagrin of the farmers. In daylight hours they congregate on a wooden post, descending with the dew at night to eat their fill of stems and leaves.

This grasshopper, harmless to farmers, looks very much like a locust and is a member of the same family. A swarm of locusts is in fact an aggregation of certain migratory grasshoppers.

These beetles and others of their kind are native to Israel and common to orchards and forests, which their larvae destroy by burrowing under the bark of trees.

that the blind shrimp has an inordinate attachment to its native spring, and that it cannot survive even the slightest alteration in the combination of temperature and salinity that go to make up its environment.

Moving from the exotic and rare to the commonplace, we come to the insects, and to make our task easier we will confine ourselves to some of those mentioned in the Bible. The best description in ancient literature of the habits of an insect is that of the locust (*Schistocerca gregaria*) in the Book of Joel:

'For a nation is come up upon my land, strong, and without number, whose teeth are the teeth of a lion, and he hath the cheek teeth of a great lion. He hath laid my vine waste, and barked my fig tree: he hath made it clean bare, and cast it away; the branches thereof are made white. Lament like a virgin girded with sackcloth for the husband of her youth. The meat offering and the drink offering is cut off from the house of the Lord; the priests, the Lord's ministers, mourn. The field is wasted, the land mourneth; for the corn is wasted: the new wine is dried up, the oil languisheth.' (Joel 1: 6–10) — and — 'A fire devoureth before them; and behind them a flame burneth: the land is as the garden of Eden before them, and behind them a desert wilderness; yea, and nothing shall escape them. And the appearance of them is as the appearance of horses; and as horsemen, so shall they run. Like the noise of chariots on the tops of mountains shall they leap, like the noise of a flame of fire that devoureth the stubble, as a strong people set in battle array. Before their face the people shall be much pained: all faces shall gather blackness. They shall run like mighty men; they shall climb the wall like men of war; and they shall march every one on his ways, and they shall not break their ranks: neither shall one thrust another; they shall walk every one in his path: and when they fall upon the sword, they shall not be wounded. They shall run to and fro in the city; they shall run upon the wall, they shall climb upon the houses; they shall enter in at the windows like a thief. The earth shall quake before them; the heavens shall tremble: the sun and the moon shall be dark, and the stars shall withdraw their shining . . .' (Joel 2:3–10).

This account attests not only to the prophet's literary gifts but also to the hold this creature had upon the imagination of the Hebrews. Even today, when there is highly efficient international cooperation for the exchange of information on the reproduction and movements of the locust, and man is equipped with very effective means of control, a swarm of locusts is still regarded as a very real and present danger. Accounts of the last great locust invasion in 1915 are no less frightening than the description given by Joel. Without going into zoological detail, there is nothing that we can add to it.

The locust is a frightening and unwelcome visitor. On the other hand, it has a number of relatives which are permanent residents in Israel without being considered pests. The species of carnivorous grasshoppers are regarded as friends of the farmer, and so is the praying mantis (*Mantis religiosa*). The desert relatives of the praying mantis have evolved a wonderful camouflage that makes them almost invisible in their native landscape.

Butterflies, and especially moths, are seen flying hither and thither, but are best known for the damage they cause in the caterpillar stage. Ever since man first laid hand to plough, the unhappy farmer has lost a sizeable share of his crop to these pests. With the industrialization of agriculture, they have become a public enemy. In Israel, as in most industrialized countries, the farmers turned on their fast multiplying foes with sprays and powders, but succeeded in achieving the exact opposite of their intention; in fact they killed the natural enemies of the pests. So the field was left open to those insects — chiefly butterflies — which were able to develop a resistance to the chemical insecticides, and the country is now full of these pests.

This does not mean that we do not have some perfectly magnificent specimens, or that our moths have nothing to offer, such as the group of large and beautiful sphinx-moths. Among the butterflies, the most outstanding are the swallowtail, the cabbage white and the red admiral.

Wild bees frequented the Land of Israel long before man put out his first hive, and the first domesticated bees (*Apis melifera*) were no less aggressive, and their sting no less painful, than the wild variety. There is therefore no point in inquiring whether the bees that Samson found in the body of the dead lion were part of a wild swarm, or domesticated bees which had left their hives in Timnah, where his bride Delilah came from. Bee-keeping is an ancient and honoured occupation in this country, and in the courtyards of Arab villages earthenware jars serving as beehives can be found with shapes unchanged since Biblical times. Just across the way, in the Jewish settlement down the road, you will find the latest bee-keeping techniques, using Italian-American crossbred bees and electrically driven honey extractors. The

This wingless desert insect, Eremia-phila, *mimics the pebbles around it so successfully that it is lost to the eye the moment it ceases to move.*

A scorpion, of which there are fifteen or more species in Israel. Generally living under stones, they can be seen almost all over the country, looking out for their prey.

Many destructive beetles, or more exactly their larvae, wreak havoc on trees and crops, as does this specimen, a pest of fruit trees.

below: *The oleander sphinx-moth, one of a group of large moths whose caterpillars compete with them in size and colour.*

above: *Colourful butterflies fill the air in spring, when they cross the country in their millions on their migratory flights.*

above: *The queen bee lays her eggs, surrounded by workers. Bees play their part in justifying the ancient description of Israel as a land flowing with milk and honey.*

right: *The dragonfly follows man and cattle along the streams and in the marshlands.*

left: *The caterpillar of the swallow-tail feeds on a noxious smelling plant, but this does not detract from the ultimate beauty of the butterfly.*

left: A glimpse of the breath-taking sights beneath the waters of the Red Sea, where hundreds of species of fish and other creatures find food and shelter in the world of the corals.

Hated by man, and for good reasons, the scorpion arches its sting-bearing tail over its back like a banner, ever at the ready to launch its poison into its enemies.

honey, whether from orange or eucalyptus blossoms or from wild flowers, is of an exquisite flavour, justifying the ancient description of Israel as a 'land flowing with milk and honey.'

An insect which played an important role in the history of Israel is the anopheles mosquito (*Anopheles*), carrier of malaria. It can be blamed for innumerable graves, children that failed to reach manhood, villages that were deserted — all because of a small insect. In its defence it might be said that the mosquito is not directly responsible for malaria, and that it is only the unwitting carrier of the microscopic *Plasmodium*, which is a parasite in its own body. This fine distinction does not carry very much weight, of course: it was the mosquito that took malaria with it wherever it went, with disastrous results. At the peak of its cultivation in former times, the Land of Israel was well-drained by man-made channels, and the water collected in this way was used for irrigation. When the country was overrun by various conquerors the irrigation system fell into disuse, and the water then became stagnant, forming swamps which were a perfect breeding place for the anopheles mosquito. Malaria sapped the strength of whole provinces and condemned entire villages to a lingering death. The few who were spared fled their homes, and their stories of the ravages of the terrible disease spread dread among all who heard them. During the latter part of the 19th century, there were large swamp areas devoid of settlement. The owners of the land were only too glad to get rid of it, and this is how the first Jewish settlers came to drain the swamps and establish their farms on the reclaimed land.

Malaria took its toll also among the pioneer Jewish settlers, affecting hundreds. As recently as the 'twenties and 'thirties of this century, there were localities in the

The centipede, whose legs do not reach the total implied by its name, is harmless to man, its poison being strong enough only to threaten insects.

Beth Shean and Hula valleys where an incidence of 200 per cent was recorded; this means that each settler fell ill with the disease on an average of at least twice during the year under review. But a determined fight was put up against the scourge. Through the draining of the swamps, and direct action against the mosquitoes themselves, the authorities succeeded in completely eradicating the anopheles strain, and by the mid-1950's the campaign had shown its worth; Israel was registered as being entirely free of malaria. There are still places where it is advisable to sleep under netting, but only for comfort; it is possible to have a sleepless night from an ordinary mosquito too.

We will spare the reader a description of the many insect pests which used to infest the country, from the common house fly down to the third and fourth plagues of Pharaoh (lice and swarms of flies). Today, we can sit back and study them with scientific detachment — or ignore them altogether. Not so long ago, however, they were an unwelcome escort to every resident and every tourist, accompanying him wherever he went. No traveller of the past could fail to mention the clouds of flies which circled over every dish, or settled on the neglected children with their open sores and running eyes. Today, only a few sightless old people remain from an earlier generation to remind us that blindness caused by flies was once very much part of everyday life.

When we think only of the creatures which dwell on land, we make the common mistake of equating insects or arthropods with the term 'invertebrate'. The mistake is easy to understand; there are infinitely more species of insect than there are snails and worms and other invertebrates. This is not the case, however, when we go down into the sea; especially the Red Sea, but the Mediterranean as well.

One of the creatures for which the Land of Israel was known in ancient times was the murex, a snail from which purple dye was extracted. Along the sea coast between

An uninvited guest that remained to become a pest; the larvae of the fig beetle feed upon trees of the fig family. Brought into Israel in timber from abroad, they spread and ruined whole orchards of fig trees.

Haifa and Tyre at the time of the Phoenicians, the Tribe of Asher followed a unique occupation — the extraction of dye from the body of this gastropod. The dye produced was the famous royal purple, associated with majesty and nobility.

The Mediterranean coast cannot boast a great abundance of living creatures. Most of the shoreline is sandy and not conducive to marine wild life. Inlets and rocky spits are few, and the islands are small and far apart. The coast of the Levant will be disappointing to anyone who has had the opportunity of visiting a marine aquarium in Italy or France. The southern sea, the Gulf of Aqaba, presents an entirely different picture; it is an offshoot of the Red Sea, and only one step removed from the Indian Ocean. Its very special climate and its direct outlet to the rich tropical life of the Indian Ocean combine to create a marvellous underwater world, full of life and colour beyond description.

190

The Gulf of Aqaba is long, narrow, deep and calm. The salinity is the highest anywhere in the open sea. It is a kind of 'appendix' to the Red Sea. The connection between them, through the Straits of Tiran, is a shallow and narrow passage, though this does not apparently interfere with the free movement of all kinds of marine life, from plankton to sharks and giant turtles. But the most beautiful of the attractions it has to offer are centred around the coral beach of Eilat.

Running parallel to the shore, some distance out in the water, is a coral reef. It is not one continuous ridge, nor is it as wide as the Great Barrier Reef of Australia. At most points, the sea bed descends steeply to great depths, so that as a rule there is only a very narrow stretch, measuring a few dozen yards, where conditions favour reef formation. Between the coral and the beach there are shallow waters, and the edge of the reef descends sharply eastwards into the depths of the sea. It is in the shallows that marine life abounds, with the coral serving as shelter and providing the staple food which initiates and renews the whole life cycle.

These creatures, which to the untrained eye often assume the appearance of plant life, are indisputably animals, members of the group of coelenterates. The wide range of colours and shapes that they assume is an indication of the vast number of species to be found. Most of them are stone corals (Hexacoralia), with a minority of soft corals (Octocoralia). The stone corals usually have a hard stony skeleton. Using their tentacles and mouths to strain the sea water, they extract particles of organic matter from which they nourish their bodies. A chemical process provides them with the calcium salts they need to build their skeletons. The offspring grow up alongside their elders, producing the various intricate shapes of the coral colony: brain, mushroom, tree, branch and so on.

Anyone who has dived into the narrows off the coral beach at Eilat and swum along under water can testify to the almost indescribably beautiful colours and shapes to be found there, the stillness broken only by the visual whisper of life. The corals are the glory of the sea, as well as the source of sustenance. Multitudes of marine creatures find shelter among them, and not only shelter but food. There are those that literally eat parts of them, setting off the predator-prey cycle. This is not the moment to look at the fish of the Red Sea, but it should be mentioned here that some of the most beautiful species are life partners with the corals, or with their relatives the sea anemones. A certain fish, the amphiprion, for example, makes its abode with a sea anemone (*Steichactis*). This anemone reaches a diameter of sixteen inches, has a mouth four inches wide and spreads its tentacles out some eight inches. The fish, with its twin stripes, rarely goes any distance away from its host, and the two parties maintain a harmonious symbiotic relationship.

Another happy couple are the sea lily (*Capillaster*), a member of the phylum Echinodermata, and the little fish *Lepadichtys*. The fish partner is quite new to

Butterflies, belonging to hundreds of different species, spend their few days of adult life fluttering from flower to flower in search of nectar.

science and was discovered and identified only during the 1960's. Details of its symbiotic relationship with the sea lily were published only recently. Much better known is the hermit crab, which makes its abode in empty conch shells on which a sea anemone lives. These 'hermits' abound in the waters off Eilat and Aqaba. The other representatives of the arthropods are the crayfish, crabs and shrimps.

There is also a wide variety of clams and snails. The largest snail has seven spines, as long as fingers, projecting from the edge of its shell, and the biggest of the clam shells reach a diameter of twenty inches. Chitons and limpets can be found clinging to the rocks, like some of the snails, while others dig themselves into the sand or under the rocks, or are scattered among the coral. The squid and the octopus, which also abound here, belong to another branch of the phylum Mollusca, as do the barnacles which cling to the rocks.

An essential precaution for anyone entering the waters of the Gulf of Aqaba is to beware of sea urchins, members of the phylum Echinodermata. The penalty for taking this warning lightly is severe. Some sea urchins, with long black spines, dig in between the stones and embed themselves in the coral reef. If an intruder is unlucky enough to tread upon one of the spines the sharp point breaks off under the skin, and the galling slime in which it is sheathed causes sharp local pain. These spines attain a length of eight inches, and each sea urchin has hundreds. As well as this particular variety of sea urchin there are others, with thicker duller spines which do not prick.

The other representatives of this phylum, the starfish, serpent star, sea cucumber and sea lily, are all to be found in great abundance. They thrive in highly saline waters, finding the environment very much to their taste.

After dark it is the turn of the luminous fish, the various jellyfish, and the serpent stars, spreading their long tentacles, to gleam and glimmer in the water, and so this silent world is in constant change throughout every hour of the twenty-four.

'Now the serpent was more subtil than any beast of the field which the Lord God had made.'

(Genesis 3:1)

UPON THY BELLY SHALT THOU GO

The serpent is almost the first creature to be mentioned by name in the Bible. This is not surprising as the serpent had held a special significance throughout the Orient, from the earliest times. It was worshipped, feared and hated, and the account in Genesis gives some indication of its special character. It is in this primeval role that it appears in the countless paintings on the subject of Adam and Eve in the Garden of Eden. But in fact it is no different from the other reptiles: like them, it emerges from the egg, lives, and dies. Yet it is a wonderfully mysterious creature, appearing suddenly and just as suddenly vanishing, implying a completely different mode of progression. Apart from the great beasts of prey, and certain insects, it is the only creature capable of killing a man, and that in one swift strike.

We speak of 'a' snake, but there are at least thirty-five different species of snake in Israel — and most of them are no more dangerous than a piece of rope of similar length. We will leave the snakes for the moment and come back to them again after dealing as a whole with the class to which they belong: the reptiles.

This land appears to be an ideal habitat for reptiles, and there are more than eighty different species, scattered throughout the country's various climatic regions. Sea turtles are to be found on the Mediterranean coast, and snakes and water turtles along the water courses. The green lizard (*Lacerta trilineator*) and other reptiles inhabit the woodlands, and the gecko makes its home among the rocks, while the harduns favour the open spaces, and the desert might have been set aside as a paradise for these creeping, crawling, gliding, cold-blooded creatures.

Everyone knows the chameleon's ability to change colour. Less well-known is its agility. Even baby ones are good climbers (below), *and for the adult* (right) *a branch, a wire, everything is a highway.*

There is a very wide variety of shapes and sizes among the reptiles of Israel. There can be no greater contrast among the mammals than, say, between the slender, darting snake and the cumbersome, slow-moving tortoise, with its deliberate movements and massive armour plate.

The tortoises and turtles, in fact, are in a group unto themselves amongst the reptiles, differing completely from all the others. The seven species in Israel are divided into three kinds of sea turtle, two fresh-water turtles, and two kinds of tortoise which dwell on land; of the two tortoises, one is rare and the other quite common.

The bridled skink has weak legs, but if it cannot escape its enemies by running at least it can slip from their clutches with the aid of its smooth skin.

The great sea turtles spend their entire lives in the sea and, except for a brief period in their reproductive cycle, they do not need dry land at all. This may seem strange because they were originally land animals, and chose water as their element. The female comes ashore once a year on a summer night and laboriously makes her way some scores of yards up the sandy beach, her webbed feet serving as paddles to push her heavy body forward. When she finds a suitable spot, she scrapes out a deep hole and there lays several dozen white eggs, in size and shape exactly like ping-pong balls. When she has finished she covers them with sand and paddles back to the sea, leaving twin tracks behind her like a tank. Unless they fall victim to some jackal prowling the beach in search of just such a delicacy, the eggs will hatch in the moist sand after sixty days. One of nature's marvels is the sight of a host of tiny turtles all crawling in one direction, towards the water. No obstacle can divert them from their objective; some hidden power seems to draw them straight towards the sea. Those which survive to maturity will crawl ashore in their turn some summer's night to lay their eggs. While science cannot give a definite answer, there is evidence that they return to the very beach on which they hatched out.

In the streams lived (and some live still) another kind, the soft shelled turtle (*Trionyx triunguis*), large, and protected only by a soft, green shell. Heavy and slow-moving as it appears on land, it is a first-rate swimmer and with its long neck it can stretch out and grab any passing fish it chooses. Inhabiting the same kind of surroundings, but much more common, is the marsh turtle (*Clemmys caspica*). They can be seen in great numbers, sunning themselves in the mud near fishponds, or on the banks of streams, and in the Hula nature reserve.

There is nothing special to be said about the common tortoise (*Testudo graeca*), simply because it is so much like those found in other countries. It should be noted only that the rarer species was discovered, or rediscovered, as recently as the 1960's.

The green lizard changes colour with age: the young one has two black stripes which it will lose as an adult.

Turning to the lizards, the Squamata, we come first to the chameleon (*Chamaeleo chamaeleon*). There is no similarity between the animal which bears this name in America and the chameleon of the Middle East. The former is simply a green tree-lizard. The true chameleon is a peculiar creature. Its paw resembles a hand, with clearly defined and articulated fingers, and it can even grasp things as in a little fist. Its protruding eyes revolve independently in their sockets in all directions. This small creature has two special characteristics. The best-known is its ability to change colour. It has been demonstrated that these 'magic' powers are limited to the green-brown-grey-white range, though some people have tried, unsuccessfully, to make the chameleon change to red or blue.

If the chameleon had to pursue its prey, it would quickly die of hunger, because its diet consists of insects far quicker than itself though, fortunately, not quicker than its tongue. When the chameleon comes within eight inches of its prey it stops, fixes its victim with its bulge-eyed stare and unleashes its tongue in a single lightening move. Before the unfortunate insect knows what is happening, it is held tightly to the sticky tip of the tongue and on its way to the chameleon's throat.

Before passing on to the rest of the reptiles, we should stop for a moment and consider a characteristic common to all of them; their cold-bloodedness. The term is not altogether accurate, since their blood is not really cold but, as distinct from birds and mammals, it does not maintain a constant temperature within the body. While, in theory, a reptile's blood temperature could thus fall to 32° F (0° C) or rise to 150° F (72° C) — the possible range in the Negev between a cold winter's night and a hot summer's day in the sun — in practice such extremes would prove fatal. Instead, when twilight comes, the reptiles, whether they be snakes or lizards, hurry away to some sheltered spot, under a stone or in a clump of earth, where the change in temperature will be less drastic. The first light of morning finds them

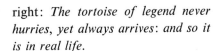
right: *The tortoise of legend never hurries, yet always arrives: and so it is in real life.*

The pale ruderate agama seeks refuge in the shade during the heat of the day, but roams the desert in the cooler hours.

practically incapable of stirring, but as time passes they begin to crawl about, seeking the sun's warmth. The warmer they grow, the more active they become. As noon draws near, and the mercury climbs into the nineties, the reptiles are at their most active. From this point on, danger threatens them again. As the temperature continues to rise they begin to lose strength, with certain death as the result of over-exposure. Of course the reptiles do not dally until the last moment, but seek out some shelter from the sun where they can pass the hottest hours. At noon there is hardly a lizard to be seen in the open desert. All are hidden — in the shade of a bush, under a stone or in a rat's hole, waiting for the cooler hours of the day, or even for the night. Incidentally, when they are warmest, and also during the mating season, some of the reptiles show that chameleons are not the only reptiles which can change their colour. There are harduns which even surpass the chameleon in the variety of shades of yellow, reddish-brown and blue which they can assume.

In common parlance, any reptile which walks on four legs and drags its tail behind it is known as a lizard. But the most cursory glance at the lizards of Israel will show that they fall into several clearly defined groups, and even everyday language must make some distinction between them. The largest lizard is the desert monitor (*Varanus*), up to four feet long. This giant makes its home in the sands between Tel Aviv and the expanses of the Negev, preying upon smaller lizards and mice. Anyone trying to catch one with the naked hand can expect a deep, painful bite.

Next in size are the agamas or harduns. Though desert dwellers, they do not necessarily confine themselves to the sands. The two species of dabb-lizard, both harduns, inhabit the most arid parts of the Negev. The Egyptian dabb-lizard (*Uromastyx*), which reaches a length of two feet and can give a nasty fright to inexperienced hikers, is popularly called the crocodile of the desert. During the chill hours of the day it is grey. Its movements are slow and it stays close to its burrow. As the temperature rises it turns yellow, straightens up on its legs and darts swiftly about. But there is nothing to fear; this creature is a vegetarian and is frightened by any living thing. Its small relative, the ornate dabb-lizard, a much rarer creature, lives among the granite and sandstone hills. Specialists maintain that, with its rich colours, it is the most handsome of the reptiles.

right: *The poisonous carpet viper of the stony desert, similar in colouring to the area in which it lives, can survive for a month or two on a single mouse, conserving its energy by moving as little as possible.*

There is nothing to fear from this young whip-snake just because it is a snake . . .

. . . and even when it grows older and longer, and changes from brown to glossy black, it is quite harmless.

The cat-snake can be recognized by its cat-like slit pupils. Otherwise it has nothing to do with cats, unless it loses to one in unequal combat.

right: *Most loathed and feared of creatures, a poisonous viper basking quietly in the grass, perhaps after a good meal.*

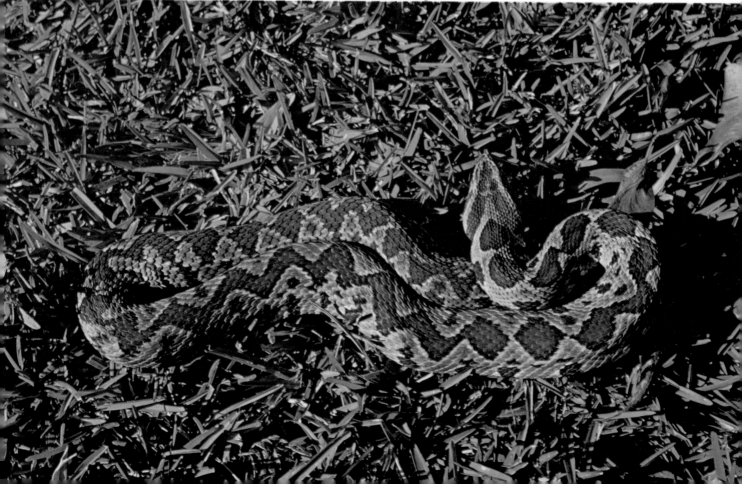

Elegant and silent, the chameleon moves undetected amongst the green leaves in search of food.

right: Know your enemy! The carpet viper can be recognized by its slit-pupilled eye, its short tail and the typical patches along its back.

In the desert of the far south the rare ornate dabb-lizard lives amongst the granite and sandstone rocks. Even when very young, as here, they show a range of colours unusual in reptiles.

The diadem snake, often taken for a viper and suffering accordingly, may hiss and bite but is a harmless, non-poisonous, creature.

Dahl's whip-snake is swift and sleek. Most common in and around human habitations, it has no venom and is completely harmless.

The soft-shelled turtle is the largest of the land turtles. Swimming in the rivers of the coastal plain, it lives on small fish.

While we are thinking about colouring amongst reptiles, the Sinai agama (*Agama sinaita*) immediately comes to mind. Its normal hue is a desert tan, but during the heat of the day and in the mating season the males take on magnificent shades of blue and copper-brown. Compared with the Sinai agama, the chameleon's ability to change colour seems very unimpressive. In addition to its beautiful colouring this agama can boast a delicacy and elegance of body and tail, with long legs to carry it swiftly across the rocky terrain. Only one species of hardun (*Agama stellio*) lives in the settled central and northern parts of the country, but it is the most widely dispersed and best known.

In contrast to the harduns, which are thick in body, and have a stiff, rough skin, the slender agile lacertid lizards are soft to the touch. They can be found in all parts of the country, from the woodlands to the desert, and each species has adapted its colouring and its habits to its particular environment. Those lizards which live in the sand or in the desert are sand-coloured, while the largest of them all, the foot-long green lizard, lives among the green forest undergrowth.

In another group are the skinks, whose smooth shiny skin is stretched tightly over their flesh. Their tiny legs are weaker than those of other lizards and they are a good example of the degeneration of the leg form in reptiles; a milestone on the road from lizard to snake.

The delicate tree frog (Hyla arborea), *only representative in Israel of a genus which prospers in the world at large; perhaps this explains its confident and overbearing tones.*

Green toads are very common where there is human habitation. In winter they fill the ponds, croaking all through the night a love song which falls hard on human ears.

As we have already said, there are some thirty-five species of snake in Israel. The smallest, the blind snake, is no more than ten inches long, while the largest, the black whip-snake, can reach eight feet. There are seven species of poisonous snake, but only one inhabits the settled areas in the northern and central parts of the country, the Palestine viper. The rest do not stray beyond the Negev and the Judean desert. All but one of the non-poisonous species live on land or in burrows in the soil. The exception is the diced water snake, which spends most of its time in the water, feeding on small fish and other water creatures. While some diced water snakes can climb trees, none of them make their homes there.

The black whip-snake (*Coluber jugularis*) is striking not only in size, but also for its deep jet colour and its swift movements when disturbed. If it sees it cannot escape it will turn on its pursuer, rise up on its coil and try to bite. Its bite is painful but not venomous. The constrictors, amongst them the largest snakes in the world, are represented in Israel by a small variety, the javelin.

The most dangerous of all the poisonous snakes in Israel is the Palestine viper (*Vipera palaestinae*), and most cases of snake poisoning, not to mention fatalities, can be traced to it. Not only does the viper inhabit just that part of the country which is most thickly settled, but it makes its home right in man's dwelling places, feeding on the mice and birds that frequent farmyards and chicken runs. Fortunately the viper, like all other native poisonous snakes, is very slow in its movements — except for its final lunge. Then it strikes like lightening. Left to itself it will not attack human beings or pursue them. Almost every case of snake bite has occurred when someone has unwittingly thrust a hand or foot too close, causing the snake to react in self-defence. When about to strike it rears up, draws its neck back and then lunges forward with its head, its mouth wide open and forward. At the same time, two fangs which are ordinarily folded back flat inside its upper jaw stand upright. As the upper jaw strikes its victim with a downward thrust, the two fangs penetrate the skin and the venom secreted by the viper's glands is injected through the narrow tubes in the fangs, just like hypodermic needles. The venom of the Palestine viper is a very unusual one, and ordinary snakebite serum is not an antidote. Only recently, after many years of research, has an effective one been developed. While the venom of the viper is no longer necessarily fatal, it is best to give them a wide berth and to avoid going barefoot after dark or poking hands or feet anywhere without looking first.

There is no single characteristic, common to the poisonous snakes alone, by which they can be readily identified, but one distinguishing feature does serve in two cases. There are two species of poisonous black snake which do live in the Negev and elsewhere, and which can be identified by their length; neither of them measures more than a yard. It follows that every short black snake, both in the Negev and elsewhere, is poisonous. The non-poisonous black whip-snake turns black only after it reaches

The bent-toed gecko is adept at mimicry; when it clings to the bark of a tree it is hardly distinguishable from it in pattern and colour.

a length of four and a half feet and does not live in the Negev. One of the two Negev dwellers, the mole viper, is indigenous only to Israel. It was identified as recently as 1942, at Ein Gedi, and its Latin name, *Atractaspis engadensis*, testifies to the fact. The other black snake from the Negev is the desert cobra, the only member of the cobra family in Israel. The rest of the poisonous snakes are Viperidae — members of the viper family — the carpet viper and the horned viper. They are all dangerous and anyone who values his life will take care to recognize and avoid them.

A mainly arid country, Israel has only a few amphibian species — seven in all, and one of these is rarely seen. The others consist of two kinds of frog, two kinds of toad and two kinds of tailed amphibians; a newt and a salamander. The croaking of the frogs in the mating season and the toads in winter is something that just cannot be ignored. It is the dominant theme on spring and winter nights. While their song may not be our idea of a lover's serenade, it has immediate results: all through the winter and spring long slimy strips of eggs begin to appear wherever there is standing water. The little tree frog (*Hyla arborea*), in contrast to others of its kind, is not repellent but even quite a likeable little creature as it climbs up a vine on the balcony, or makes a terrific leap from one end of a verandah to the other.

Only naturalists and nature lovers are acquainted with the spotted newt (*Triturus vitattus*), which passes the summer buried in mud at the bottom of dried up pools, waking only with the first rains. The salamander (*Salamandra salamandra*) is much better known, though it appears only in winter on the damp mountain sides. Because of its orange-and-black colouring and poison sacs (its venom affects only insects) it has inspired all sorts of horror tales and superstitions, none of them founded in fact. It is viviparous, bearing its young alive in mountain streams.

The amphibians, which once ruled the whole world, have shrunk in Israel to a tiny group, a pale reflection of their former glory.

'...and fowl that may fly above the earth in the open firmament of heaven.'

(Genesis 1:20)

A young stone curlew must face the dangers of the world around from the moment it is hatched, on the open ground, and follow its parents on its own two feet.

THE FOWL OF THE AIR

Opinions might differ as to whether Israel is a paradise for birds, but there can be no doubt that it is a paradise for bird-watchers. That there are 380 different species of bird to be seen in Israel may not mean very much to anyone who is unfamiliar with the subject, but this figure acquires new significance if we compare it with the number of birds which can be seen in far larger countries, and even in whole continental areas. For example, France, Britain, Spain and Japan can each boast a mere 400 to 440 different species, while Europe up to the Russian border has 577 species, Russia 700 species and the United States 725.

In an earlier chapter we explained that it is not a mere matter of chance that large numbers of birds choose to make their homes in this area, or to arrive here on their seasonal migrations. The position of Israel, at the crossroads of three continents, makes it a focal point for the feathered world, and her bird population may be divided into five groups.

Firstly come the resident birds, those which breed in this country, raise their young, and spend the whole year here, the good seasons with the bad. The inclusion of a certain species in this category should not be taken to mean that every single bird is a full time resident — a fact which could only be finally determined by ringing every bird. Second are the winter birds, which arrive between September and December and set out on their way again between February and May. They come from various European countries, where they lay their eggs and raise their young, and return there every year. In recent years, a number of species formerly thought of as winter

left: *Danger at hand! This, evidently, the young night heron felt, as it left its nest and clung to a nearby branch.*

Important event in a heron's nest, one of hundreds in a nesting colony: a chick emerges.

215

With the continuous destruction of forest trees, woodpeckers became very rare in Israel, but they are increasing in numbers after two generations of reafforestation.

birds have begun to breed here and they are now included amongst the group of residents.

Of the third group, the summer birds, the earliest arrive in Israel in February while the last to come remain until September. With the exception of one species, which comes from India, they are all from Africa, though they could all be considered natives, as they are fledged in Israel and return as adults to breed again. In fact, it is their time away from Israel which could be said to be transitory. Fourthly come the true migrants, which pass across Israel twice a year, on their way south from Europe to Africa in the autumn, and northwards again from Africa to Europe in the spring. On every passage they spend periods from a few days to a few weeks in this country. Lastly come the relatively small group of vagrants; these are unlike all the previous groups, which follow set paths or fixed timetables, and turn up in Israel only occasionally, at irregular intervals, disappearing from the scene again in the same way as they came.

Inclusion in one group or another still tells us nothing of the relative rarity or abundance of a particular species or its contribution to the local scene. A particular resident species might be quite rare, and the birds themselves well concealed and shy, like the wren (*Troglodytes troglodytes*) or the tawny owl (*Strix aluco*), while another

Thistle seeds are the favourite diet of the goldfinch, which is most often seen in summer perched on the dry thistles which abound in the countryside.

bird, included perhaps amongst the migrants, like the stork, cannot escape notice.

The composition of the feathered world changes before our eyes from season to season, not only in variety of species but in the intensity of their activity. During the two migratory seasons, the autumn and the spring, the emphasis is on the change in population; birds to which we have become accustomed are no longer to be seen, while new ones appear daily and settle in for a season. A flock of swallows (*Hirundo rustica*) will come for a day, lining the overhead wires and hopping about the farmyards and gardens. Then, on the next day, they will be gone. Newcomers can be recognized at once; those on their way vanish silently. The vast assemblies of departing migrants and their striking flight formations, so familiar in Europe, are not to be seen in Israel.

Another feature of bird life which is infinitely absorbing to the bird-watcher is the way the birds nest and minister to their young. The first eggs are laid in February and the last in August, but the peak period is in April and May, when every sort of bird may be seen on every side, all engaged in the same occupations: staking out territory, building their nests or tending their young. During the 'quiet' winter months there is an abundance of winter birds taking up residence in all kinds of places, from kitchen gardens to fishponds.

The young hooded crow has much to tell its brother: they are considered to be very clever birds and have to keep up their reputation.

As far as birds are concerned, the year is divided into several seasons: between September and December the autumn migration is taking place. At the same time some migrants are passing through, while the winter birds are still arriving to settle for a while. As we have already mentioned, the departure of the summer birds at this time passes almost unnoticed. There are places where several scores of different species can be counted within a few days. Then, between December and March, the winter birds join the resident bird population, and become the dominant factor as they hop about the fields and gardens and fly over every stretch of water. Thousands of coots (*Fulica atra*), ducks and other water fowl and an infinite number of starlings (*Sturus vulgaris*) fill the countryside, their formations crossing the sky in vast clouds.

From March until May, the spring migration overlaps the nesting. It is at this season, when the pulse of life beats strongest in every sphere, that the migration turns back upon itself, from south to north, bringing back species whose departure went almost unnoticed during their autumn passage. The nesting birds, both the resident species and the summer visitors, are at their busiest.

Flocks of migrant starlings darkened the skies as they arrived in multitudes in former years. More recently their numbers have dwindled, for reasons not yet fully determined.

The period from June to August is the only time when the birds seem to be a little subdued. We say 'a little' advisedly since, in fact, some are still nesting — particularly such waders as the spur-winged plover (*Hoplopterus spinosus*) and the black-winged stilt (*Himantopus himantopus*). The migration southwards has already begun, the first species making their move as early as July, and some in August, yet on the whole this is a quiet season in the bird world.

Space does not permit even a cursory survey of the teaming bird life of Israel, and we shall confine ourselves to a description of birds mentioned in the Bible. Even here we shall have to limit ourselves: the Bible mentions no less than thirty-five species of bird (though one of them does not concern us. Included in the list of abominated birds in Leviticus — which incidentally contains the fullest list of animal life anywhere in the Bible — is the bat, which in the opinion of the modern zoologist is not a bird. The ancient legislator apparently did not want to rely on the zoological expertise of the Hebrews and, since the bat flies and its flesh is taboo, included it in the list of prohibited birds).

Hatched in a nest dug by its parents in a steep bank of earth, this Smyrna kingfisher has now left it and takes stock of the world around.

Apart from dietary considerations, for or against, our forefathers were struck by precisely those avian characteristics which make an impression on us: their song, their nesting habits and their migrations. When the Prophet Jeremiah wanted to impress upon the people their neglect of God's commandments he likened them to birds: 'Yea, the stork in the heaven knoweth her appointed times; and the turtle and the crane and the swallow observe the time of their coming; but my people know not the judgment of the Lord.' (Jeremiah 8: 7) It may be of interest to mention that these birds have not changed their habits since the days of the prophet. To this day they are the most conspicuous amongst the migratory birds, and 'observe the time of their coming.' Also in Lamentations, Jeremiah is certainly under the mood cast by the night song of the nocturnal birds when he calls out to the daughter of Zion: 'Arise, cry out in the night: in the beginning of the watches pour out thine heart.' (Lamentations 2: 19)

Birds' nests were also the subject of one of God's commandments: 'If a bird's nest chance to be before thee in the way, in any tree, or on the ground, whether they be young ones, or eggs, and the dam sitting upon the young, or upon the eggs, thou shalt not take the dam with the young.' (Deuteronomy 22: 6)

The birds of prey — all of them prohibited as food — are accorded a central place in the biblical lists. It is an interesting sidelight that all the nocturnal birds known to us today are mentioned in the Bible. We are familiar with nine species, all members of the owl family, *Strigidae*, and of the order Strigiformes, some of which are quite rare, while others can be seen on almost any night in settled areas.

Outstanding among diurnal birds of prey is the king of birds, though here we run into a problem of identification. The bird which the Bible calls a *nesher* is generally translated as 'eagle' but the zoologists disagree. They do not dispute that in Roman and Greek tradition the eagle was the king of birds, but assert that in Israel the

The hoopoe carries its crest proudly, or so it seems, for it loses no opportunity to display it.

reference, and justifiably so, is to a bird which is not highly thought of in Europe: the griffon vulture (*Gyps fulvus*). Its taste for carrion did not prevent our forefathers from ascribing certain kingly attributes to it. Whatever our prejudices, the vulture is the largest, the most impressive and the most exalted of all the birds to be found in Israel. Until only a few years ago vultures could be seen here in their hundreds, and scores of nests dotted the niches and crannies of the mountain precipices, but modern living, with its hunters and its practice of not leaving carrion out to rot, has decimated the vulture population. Nevertheless, these great birds can still be seen occasionally, gliding across the sky or perched in isolated grandeur near their nests on the mountain sides. Two related though far rarer species may be seen in the Negev: the black vulture and the lappet-faced vulture.

There are also several species of eagle, mostly migrants or winter birds, with only one or two residents. The famous golden eagle (*Aquila chrysaetos*) calls here only very rarely, but the imperial eagle (*A. heliaca*) is fairly common. Bonelli's eagle (*Hieratus fasciatus*) is the most at home, each pair choosing a valley for its private use and chasing away every would-be interloping eagle. The bird which has made the best adjustment is the short-toed eagle (*Circaetus gallicus*), thanks to its taste for snakes. It is an unforgettable sight to see it floating over the fields, its white underside gleaming in the sunlight, before diving suddenly to grab some snake which it has spotted from on high. Holding its prey to the ground with its claw, it splits open the snake's head with its beak and swallows the still wriggling reptile whole, like spaghetti. By confining itself to a diet of snakes it has avoided the fate of other birds of prey, which have all too often fallen victim to poisoned bait set out for jackals and hyenas, or fed on poisoned rats.

A bird which has left a lasting impression on man's imagination is the stork. There are good grounds for believing that storks used to breed here in ancient times: 'as

The great days of the Saker falcon are in the past, when it was trained to hunt game.

for the stork, the fir trees are her house' (Psalms 104: 17). Occasionally a stork will experiment with laying its eggs here, but it is not usual. As a rule, they drop in upon Israel only in passing — we touched on this in an earlier chapter. It would be hard to imagine spring in Israel without storks, following along behind the ploughman and the reaper in their search for worms and insects.

Among the abominations mentioned in Leviticus are 'the heron after her kind' (11: 19), and this gives a hint of the many types of heron to be found in Israel; no less than ten in fact. They range from the Goliath heron (*Ardea goliath*) which, fully extended, is as tall as a boy, to the little bittern (*Ixobrychus minutus*). Most of them live near some stretch of water, or marshland. There are herons which make their home here, species which are migrant and others which are seasonally resident. Most of them are common to both Europe and Israel and their habits there are the same as here.

It is an interesting sight to see three or four different species of heron nesting in one colony. For the most part, cattle egrets, night herons, squacco herons and little egrets get on well together. There seems to be some kind of mutual attraction between herons, and one nesting area may appeal to several different species. They begin gathering to nest in March, generally in a dry thicket in a swamp or in some shady grove. Hundreds of them will build their nests, one next to another. The colony is at its busiest in April and May, with some of the herons sitting on their eggs, others feeding their young and, at a later stage, taking them for walks beyond the nest. There is much coming and going, flapping of wings, raucous cries and little fights, calling to mind a busy market place or a crowded city street.

The pheasant family (*Phasianidae*) has always been an object of interest in Israel: they make a tasty meal, permitted under the Jewish dietary laws. The best-known member of the family, the common chicken, is not explicitly mentioned in the Bible, though we have every reason to believe that it was already known in biblical times.

The short-toed eagle is the only bird of prey that has not suffered the consequences of exterminating rodents with poison. It feeds almost exclusively on snakes and lizards, which it spots from the air, swooping and swallowing without hesitation.

A young spur-winged plover, bred close to water. It has not yet attained to to the fine-coloured plumage of the adults.

The nest of the spur-winged plover is no more than a shallow depression on the ground. The four eggs are difficult to detect unless a glancing sunbeam catches them from the side. The adults are fierce defenders of their young.

above: *The rock partridge and its chicks are so much a part of the natural scene in Israel, it is not surprising that they figure in the mosaic floor of the ancient synagogue of Beth Alfa (sixth century AD). Subjects from nature were very common in mosaics, especially where representations of human figures, except in Bible stories, were forbidden.*

overleaf above: *Tristram's grackle, a typical resident of the rocks around the Dead Sea, gives forth wonderful song, in clear loud tones.*

overleaf below: *To build their nests, these swallows must carry quantities of mud in their beaks.*

overleaf right above: *The bulbul, with a bold and cheeky look in his eyes as he takes his choice of sweetness among the ripe dates. Of African origin, this bird is well established in Israel.*

overleaf right below: *The little owl, commonest of all the owls in Israel, is active mainly at night, but keeps an eye half-open in the daytime too.*

left: *Young night herons make their acquaintance with the world around them.*

The vulture, not the eagle, is regarded in Israel as the king of birds. Here it raises its head proudly and surveys its domain.

Cranes are not common in Israel, but they flock in hundreds to a few places where they find fields near lakes. Their flight, in arrowhead formations, is unforgettable.

For example, a seal found north of Jerusalem bearing the imprint 'Leiozniahu, servant of the King', is decorated with a handsome portrait of a cockerel. Three of the four species of pheasant found in Israel are mentioned in the Bible: the quail, the desert partridge and the rock partridge.

The songbirds, the largest group in the feathered kingdom, are represented in appropriate numbers amongst the birds of Israel — although not in the Bible. Only three of the hundred and forty members of the order to be found here are mentioned: the nightingale, the sparrow and the crow. We have no way of knowing if our forefathers even had a name for every bird, but there is no reason to doubt that the species we see today were also inhabitants of the land in biblical times.

Zoologists classify all the songbirds together. The layman, on the other hand, finds it difficult to accept the grouping of the great black raven (*Corvus corax*) together with the tiny goldcrest (*Regulus regulus*). From its habits the raven would seem to belong with the birds of prey and, on the quality of its song, it certainly would not pass muster as a songbird. However, the zoologists have thought otherwise, and included it among the species of songbirds. In Israel these fall into five categories of residence habit, some species being quite rare while others are common all over the country.

Only very few gulls breed on the small rocky islands off the coast of Israel, but multitudes arrive in winter as migrants, and find good fishing along the shore and in the fishponds.

'Every raven after his kind', as the Bible has it, covers a number of highly distinctive representatives. There are two varieties of great black raven, one in the north and the other in the Negev. The southern variety makes its home in the wide expanses of the desert, generally flying in pairs, their large size and their jet black plumage standing out in the barren wastes. When the Prophet Elijah hid by the brook of Cherith (I Kings 17: 3) the Lord ordered the ravens to feed him, and they brought him 'bread and flesh in the morning, and bread and flesh in the evening . . .' The black ravens which to this day inhabit the holes and crannies in the rock along this ravine could perform the same task with ease, even without instructions from on high; they are often to be seen carrying quite large chunks of meat in their beaks.

Up until a few years ago, the winter skies would be darkened by vast flocks of crows, particularly the hooded crow (*Corvus corone sardonius*) and the jackdaw (*Corvus monedula*). Lately, however, they have become far scarcer for some unknown reason. They are no longer seen at all in winter, and only the small native population which always nested here has remained. The hooded crows build their nests in familial privacy, each pair in their own tree, while the jackdaws nest in colonies.

A member of the family worth mentioning here, although not a true raven, is the jay (*Garrulus glandarius*). They inhabit the woodlands and orchards of the hill

Young rufous warblers, not singing in a choir but waiting for their parents to bring them food.

regions and are best known for their black, white and blue plumage and their clamourous cawing.

The nightingale is mentioned by name in the original Hebrew of the Bible (Song of Solomon 2: 12), though the Authorized Version speaks only of 'the singing of birds'. Nightingales can only be found now in the Jordan Valley in springtime, spinning their famous song through the evening hours.

The house sparrow, or English sparrow as it is known in America, is the most common bird in Israel. Its very name in Latin, *Passer domesticus biblicus*, clearly indicates its affinity to the country. A related species, far more colourful and much less common, is the Spanish sparrow (*Passer hispaniolensis*). But undoubtedly the most interesting of the genus is the Dead Sea sparrow, which has already been mentioned in an earlier chapter on its natural habitat, the Jordan Valley. This species is confined to the Middle East, and its most distinctive feature is the enormous egg-shaped nest it builds, a foot in diameter and more than three pounds in weight, cunningly constructed entirely from twigs.

We will conclude the chapter with a description of a bird which, even though it may not be mentioned in the Bible, has a special association with the country — the Palestine sunbird (*Cinnyris osea osea*). The smallest birds in Israel, they can hover easily in one spot. The males are blue-black in colouring and the females grey, and they have long slender curved beaks. The bird literature of the beginning of this century described the sunbird as being extremely rare, and there is even a dramatic account of how the famous zoologist Aharoni went out to capture a pair of sunbirds in the groves near Jericho as a gift for the Turkish sultan. Today, perhaps because gardening has become more popular, affording a wider choice of habitat, Palestine sunbirds have become quite common, and are frequent visitors in every garden, where their hovering and chirruping are familiar to all Israelis.

'Knowest thou the time when the wild goats of the rock bring forth? or canst thou mark when the hinds do calve?'

(Job 39:1)

A young jackal can be tamed like a puppy, but when it grows older the primitive instincts of a wild animal predominate.

BEASTS OF THE FIELD

It is easier to be a mouse in an inhabited land than a lion. This tragic truth was learned the hard way by most of the larger animals which once dwelt in the Holy Land, and few of them are now left to tell the tale; the rest have simply been wiped out and have completely vanished. Of the scores of kinds of mammals which lived in the area in recorded time, many are no longer to be seen and, among those that still remain, many are so reduced in numbers that they are in real danger of extinction. Even so, with a little bit of luck or, failing that, a good guide, many of the animals mentioned in the Bible may still be found in their natural habitat.

The Bible mentions thirty species of wild mammals, as well as ten domestic ones. Zoologists know now of about eighty species of wild mammals, but that number is meaningless without looking into further details. More than half of the total are bats and mice; of the others, some exist in very small numbers and can be seen only on very rare occasions.

Most mammals are diurnal beasts by nature, and if some have become nocturnal prowlers it is generally from fear of man, so that most daylight animals, now, are either especially swift, or ingenious hiders, or else live in areas not generally frequented by man.

Of the herbivores, three large ones still remain to be found: the Nubian ibex, the gazelle and the wild boar, forbidden food for both Jews and Moslems. The ibex is strictly a mountain animal; in the words of the Psalmist (104: 28): 'The high hills are a refuge for the wild goats.' (As already explained in Chapter four, the translation in the Authorized Version from the Hebrew names is not always in agreement with current scientific identification of the animals. In this book the animals are identified in accordance with current knowledge, which appears sometimes to conflict with the passages quoted from the Bible.)

While the ibex (*Capra ibex nubiana*) may once have frequented hill country inhabited by man, they have long since taken refuge in the desert. The ease with which they scale the steepest cliffs amazes every observer. At the end of some desert wadi, locked between two sheer rock walls, you may come upon a small herd of ibex — he-goat, a few nannies and some kids. The he-goat has enormous horns, sometimes reaching a yard or more in length. Curving backwards, they are thick at the base and knotted in front. As if to lend dignity to his appearance, he sports a beard under his chin. The nannies are somewhat smaller and their horns are much shorter, without the frontal knots. Amongst the kids, some still show no sign of horns but others are beginning to sprout them, so that it is already possible to distinguish the males.

The male gazelle carries these splendid horns throughout its adult life, unlike the deer, which shed their antlers every year. The horns are mainly used in fights between males during the rutting season.

For the ancient Hebrews the female gazelle was a symbol of beauty and love, and this is the meaning of the Hebrew and Arabic names for this animal.

They have not seen you yet, and continue to graze contentedly, moving slowly on from bush to bush, nibbling at a leaf here and there. But one pair of eyes is sure to be on the look-out while all the rest of the herd are peacefully engaged in filling their bellies. One careless movement on the part of the still unobserved intruder, perhaps a pebble dislodged by an unguarded step, and the whole scene changes in a flash. If the distance between herd and danger is great enough, or if they feel secure in their terrain, the ibex make away gracefully up the side of the wadi, taking advantage of every niche and foothold in a way that would make any commando sergeant green with envy. But if they are startled by someone quite close or, worst of all, by someone who comes upon them from above, the he-goat lets out a sharp whistling sound, completely unlike the normal bleating of goats, and the entire herd scampers up the cliff. Anyone who had never seen a herd of ibex climbing up the sheer face of a mountain gorge would find it hard to believe that any four-footed animal could make such an ascent. The ibex can leap two or three yards straight upwards from a foothold no bigger than a crack in the rock. Only when the entire herd has reached the summit do they halt, looking back and downwards with a slightly stupid but defiant gaze.

The he-goats use their horns for one purpose only; combat with other males. No male ibex worth his salt feels at peace with himself unless he has a harem of at least several nannies. But for this, he must fight. Two he-goats will duel, lunging at each other with their horns till the very valleys echo with the sound of battle. The victor gets the nanny, and the loser joins the society of the vanquished, who herd together with those who have not yet reached mating age and those who have passed their prime, in groups of up to thirty head. With their massive horns and dignified beards, they make an impressive sight in the desert.

The ibex was regarded as a symbol of beauty by the people of ancient times. Witness the 'pleasant roe' of Proverbs (5: 19), an expression to describe a beautiful girl in Hebrew to this day. The name Jael (*ibex*) has been a popular one from the time of Jael, wife of Heber the Kenite, down to the present. The ibex had long been in danger of extinction from the firearms of Bedouins in the Negev, but in recent years, following the promulgation of nature conservation laws by the State of Israel, they are once again growing plentiful, and their herds are one of the many wonders of the desert.

'The rocks of the wild goats in the wilderness of En-Gedi' appear in Samuel I (24: 1–2). This place, where David and his men hid from the wrath of Saul, is still a grazing ground for herds of ibex. Scores of them are to be found in every wadi, nimbly scaling the cliff walls and peering down at passers-by from on high.

If the ibex is king of the rocks, then the gazelle (*Gazella gazella*) reigns over the plains and hills: 'Until the day break, and the shadows flee away, turn, my beloved,

and be thou like a roe or a young hart upon the mountains of Bethel (Song of
Solomon 2: 17). This shy wild thing is not found in Europe and America, and many
of the early biblical commentators confused the gazelle (*tsvi*) with the roe deer
(*ayal*), with which they were more familiar. There were deer in Israel at one time,
but they are no longer to be seen, while there are gazelles aplenty.

Our ancestors had good reason to see the gazelle as another symbol of beauty
and love. No one observing this light-footed animal with its proud neck and slender
legs, and the gentle expression upon its face, could think otherwise.

The gazelle favours open spaces, leaving the cliffs and peaks to the ibex and the
wooded areas to the deer. Here it was born, in the open field amid the lush grass, and
not in a cave or a lair. The fawn is able to walk a few hours after birth, but generally
spends its first days in the shade of a bush in the field, with its mother hovering a
little distance away and coming every few hours to give suck. After a few days it
begins to follow her about, and by the time it is two or three weeks old it is already
running swiftly enough to be difficult to catch. The fawns graze in open country with
their mothers for most of the summer, and by autumn are already showing the
rudiments of horns: the females grow slender, straight horns and the males thicker
ones, formed ring upon ring and curved in a lyre-shape. The males begin to fight

below: *The honey badger makes rare appearances, but worthy of its name, turning beehives upside down in search of honey.*

above: *The spiny mouse is one of the few diurnal animals of the desert, darting among the rocks in search of snails: it needs no water.*

above: *Small but fierce is the marbled polecat, perhaps the most colourful of Israel's mammals, hunter of rats in the fields.*

below: *The hedgehog is not just a ball of prickles, but an inquisitive little animal, as may be seen from its face.*

each other in single combat to choose their mates, and so the herds are gradually formed for the winter; a buck surrounded by several does in one group and a number of bachelor bucks in the others. While a herd of gazelles running through a field of wheat is not likely to endear itself to farmers, their grace is nevertheless a wonderful thing in itself. When the author of the Book of Samuel wanted to say how swiftly Asahel could run, he said that he 'was as light of foot as a wild roe.' (II Samuel 2: 18), while in I Chronicles 12: 7 the 'men of might' who fought with David were said to be 'as swift as the roes upon the mountains.' One of the names by which the Land of Israel was known was *Eretz-Hatsvi*, 'land of the gazelle.'

We turn now from one of the most delicate and best-loved of wild animals to one of the clumsiest and least attractive, the wild boar (*Sus scrofa*). It may come as a surprise to many, and especially to those who are better acquainted with its domesticated brother, that students of animal psychology have found the boar has one of the highest levels of intelligence of any wild animal. This of course explains how this combination of pest and game animal has managed to survive in proximity to man throughout the centuries.

The wild boar has always been notorious as a nuisance to farmers: 'The boar out of the wood doth waste it, and the wild beast of the field doth devour it' (Psalms 80: 13). The damage it causes is not only in what it consumes but also, and chiefly, in what it tramples upon and crushes in its passage. In the course of time, the encroachments of man drove the boars to seek refuge in the depths of marshlands, and the biblical expression 'The boar out of the wood . . .' became more or less meaningless. With the draining of the swamps in more recent times, however, they have migrated back to the forests and to the hills. In their contacts with man they display extraordinary caution, and only the most experienced hunters manage to track them down, even when their closeness cannot be doubted. Their ability to multiply rapidly has also stood them in good stead in their war against extermination.

The piglets are usually born during the first week of April. Their coats are mottled, with yellow stripes on a greyish-brown background. The colouring bears a remarkable resemblance to the thickets in which they dwell, and so affords the maximum camouflage. The male, with his sharp tusks, can be seen escorting a line of piglets waddling after their mother, and is prepared to defend them with his life. Within a few months the young lose their yellow stripes, and with them their special privileges in wild pig society. So long as they are still striped, no adult boar will do them harm, even if provoked. Once they too enter adult estate, they have to find their own level in the herd, to fight for their food and even for their lives.

They particularly like irrigated fields and swampland. They can do considerable damage to a cornfield or a banana plantation, crushing underfoot with their 300-pound bulk whatever they do not uproot to eat. They feel at home too, in thickets

above: *When the mosaic floor at Beth Gubrin was laid, during the Byzantine period, lions still roamed the land and were a familiar subject for the artist.*

below: *A rabbit feeding on grapes, as depicted in the mosaic floor of the ancient synagogue at Beth Alfa.*

The mighty natural fortress of Masada stands on guard over the generations in the Judean Desert, where herds of camels are as eternal as the rock.

right: *A young male ibex scans the desert from a vantage point. At the slightest sign of danger it scales the steep cliffs so nimbly that no enemy can reach it.*

above: *The hedgehog, though spiny like the herbivorous porcupines, is not related to them, but is in fact an insectivore, feeding mainly on insects.*

This charming small mammal is a dormouse, of which there are two species in Israel, one a denizen of the woods and the other a desert dweller.

in wooded areas and in fruit orchards in the hilly regions, where they also cause a lot of harm. As already mentioned, their flesh is forbidden both to Jews and to Moslems.

Turning to the smaller herbivorous mammals, the largest is the porcupine (*Hystrix indica*). It is a first-class burrower, with forepaws as strong as a bear's, and depends for its safety more on its burrowing ability than on its quills. Contrary to popular belief, a porcupine cannot shoot its quills at will, and in fact has no need to. All it has to do is to raise these black and white spines until they stand upright and suddenly it becomes a frightening monster which no sensible mammal would seek to challenge. Only a leopard would dare to take on an adult porcupine, while jackals are known to favour young ones which have not yet sprouted quills. Porcupines leave their burrows at night in search of vegetable patches. There they eat their fill, untroubled by the prospect of an outraged farmer's curses.

While taking his nightly dinner, the porcupine could well encounter a hare (*Lepus europaeus*). There are no wild rabbits in Israel, only field hares, which are common throughout the country. They do not dig burrows, but take refuge in the shadow of a thorn or under a rock, waiting till a pursuer is nearly upon them, leaping out suddenly and making off in a zig-zag dash before the unwanted visitor can make a move. The female nurses her young in the field as well, cradling them in a shallow hole on the ground. Every few hours she goes to give them suck, getting the job over as quickly as possible before retreating a little distance away to keep watch.

Another small mammal is the cony or hyrax (*Procavia capensis*). Found mainly in Africa and unknown in Europe, Israel and Syria are about the northernmost limit of its distribution. A cave-dweller, it has diurnal habits. If you happen to be watching at sunrise on a mountain escarpment inhabited by conies, you may be lucky enough to see the first ones come out of their holes. Their oval, brown furry bodies, with small ears and short tails, bounce along the crest of a ridge, as they nibble a blade of grass here and there and stop occasionally to take a sunbath. A seasoned male is always posted as look-out, and a warning shriek from him is enough to alert all these furry creatures and send them scurrying back to their caves. The cony is definitely not a rodent, but a distant relative of the elephant.

We will devote only a few words to one large group of mammals; mice and their kind. Several species were mentioned in passing during a description of the regions they inhabit, such as the gerbil and the spiny-mouse, which dwell in the Negev. Of them all, the field mouse or vole understandably has the worst reputation. It was already notorious in biblical times, when the Philistines were plagued by mice. The Bible does not give us details of what happened in the country of the Philistines, to convince them that they must return the Ark of the Lord as quickly as possible (I Samuel 6), accompanied by golden mice, but any farmer knows why from his own experience. Occasionally the vole is joined by some of its relatives in their

The caracal in captivity expresses fear and rage. Roaming in its native desert, it avoids encounters with man.

below: *Ichneumons are amongst the few wild mammals that are diurnal: they may be seen in daylight, crossing a road singly or in groups.*

depredations upon the crops. There are other species of mice, the dormouse and the wood mouse, less offensive to man, which do not attack fields or damage houses. They make their little holes in the ground or else build nests in trees. Everyone who sees these little animals is always charmed by their appealing ways.

And from mice — to cats. The last of the great beasts of prey still at large is the leopard, about which we have spoken earlier. The flag of the cat family is borne aloft by three animals: the wild cat, the jungle cat and the desert-dwelling caracal lynx (*Felis caracal*). The wild cat (*Felis lybica*) is a direct descendant of the holy cat, worshipped by the Egyptians, whose divinity derived from its lordship over the agelong enemy, the mouse. It is generally accepted that the wild cat is also the ancestor of the domestic cat common to the Middle East, and in fact house cats mate with the wild variety without any hesitation. The pure-bred wild cat makes its home in the wooded ravines of central and northern Israel, favouring the vicinity of settled areas. It has apparently come to the conclusion that the flesh of a chicken from the farm is no less tasty than that of a partridge, and it is here that it comes into contact with domestic cats. We are no longer surprised when we see a litter of black-and-white or tabby kittens with one which is completely yellowish-brown, striped like a tiger, with three black rings at the end of its tail, the living image of the wild cat that its mother probably met lurking behind the chicken run.

The jungle cat (*Felis chaus*) is considerably larger than the wild cat, and while it does not turn up its nose at meat, it is generally considered to prefer fish. In earlier times, this creature used to make its home in swampy undergrowth and catch its fish in the fresh-running streams. But the Jewish settlers gradually drained all the swamps, driving the jungle cat to its final refuge, the cane thickets along the banks of the Jordan River. Some experts had already added the jungle cat's name to the list of native animals which had become extinct. Then, at the last moment, salvation came from an unexpected quarter: the very people who had drained the swamps began to raise fish in ponds. The jungle cat was reprieved, with the prospect of unlimited fresh carp for a long time to come. Incidentally, cats are not mentioned in the Bible, although there can be no doubt that the Israelites were acquainted with them; there are too many Egyptian cats wherever that empire extended, including the Land of Israel. The only cats mentioned by name are the leopard and the lion.

The largest of the canines in the Holy Land is the wolf (*Canis lupus*), and in this generation they have shown themselves to be far from extinct. Until recently, shepherds were the principal victims of their depredations. They were convinced that the wolves did not make their home in Israel, but entered the country every once in a while from 'somewhere' in some neighbouring state. It has now been clearly established that this 'somewhere' does not exist, and that wolves are indigenous to Israel. Their experience with human beings during the centuries has taught them to

above: *Badgers are shy and do not show themselves in the daylight hours, which they regard as the best time for sleeping.*

A new immigrant from South America, the coypu, or nutria, was brought to Israel for its fur, but escaped and became naturalized in the wild.

*The swamp is an ideal habitat for the
wild boar, not only for the adults but
for the striped young too.*

beware of man and his doings, even if this means that they have to work harder for
their food, subsisting on small wild animals. Occasionally a pack of wolves will forget
this lesson and try to make a meal off a few goats, or even a calf or two — and they
do so at the risk of their lives. Only recently, a pack of wolves of a desert species was
found in the Negev.

The jackal and the fox have divided out the country between them. The jackal
(*Canis aureus*) inhabits the periphery of man's settlement, enjoying all the farmer's
bounty — vegetables and fruit, garbage and a stray chicken here and there. It also
pays for its strife with man, sometimes devouring the poison set out for it along with
its food. Whatever the reason, it is inseparably linked to man, even to keeping him

awake through winter nights with its howls. The fox (*Vulpes vulpes*), on the other hand, chose independence in preference to the easy life. It may sometimes be seen even during the daylight hours, prowling around the rocks with its long bushy tail stretching out behind it. In legend, the fox is endowed with cunning, and the jackal with all the most undesirable social traits. However, the zoologists think otherwise. In their opinion, the jackal displays more than ordinary intelligence in its capacity to adapt to changing circumstances and overcome the manifold dangers which surround it, whereas the fox can only claim a delicate long nose flanked by a large pair of eyes. Speaking of foxes, we are reminded of Samson: 'And Samson went and caught three hundred foxes, and took firebrands, and turned tail to tail, and put a firebrand in the midst between two tails. And when he had set the brands on fire, he let them go into the standing corn of the Philistines, and burnt up both the shocks, and also the standing corn, with the vineyards and olives.' (Judges 15: 4–5). While it might have been difficult to catch 300 jackals, to catch 300 foxes would have been impossible. Anyone familiar with the wild life of the country can only conclude that Samson's 'foxes' must really have been jackals.

One beast of prey which has had a bad name all through recorded time is the hyena (*Hyaena hyaena*). In the east, at any rate, it is more feared than the lion, and all sorts of supernatural powers are attributed to it. There are probably several reasons for this, one of them being the hyena's practice of stripping the bones of the fallen in battle. Its appearance is just about the strangest of any mammal: a massive head set on very broad shoulders and supported by sturdy forelegs, with the rest of the body looking like a kind of afterthought, held up by delicate hindlegs. Biologically speaking, its presence is quite desirable, serving as a kind of natural sanitation department by devouring any carrion, no matter how rank the smell. Hyenas are not very common in Israel, but those that there are may be found anywhere and their characteristic tracks, a large paw alternating with a small one, turn up from the north to the Negev.

In addition to these, there are perhaps ten or so smaller beasts of prey, less well-known because they are relatively rare, particularly cautious or simply nocturnal. Neither of these two last-named traits applies to the ichneumon (*Hespestes ichneumon*), however. A whole family may occasionally be seen crossing a road in broad daylight, wonderfully agile with their short legs and long tails. The marbled polecat (*Vormela peregusna*), with its trademark stripe down its back and tiny wicked teeth, makes its home in the fields, feeding voraciously on mice and staying out of the way of the ploughman. Every once in a while the fish breeders are infuriated when they come across the traces of a meal made by the otter from their ponds, the fresh fish partly eaten. On the other hand, it is almost impossible to get a glimpse of the badger (*Meles meles*). This nocturnal animal is extraordinarily

The hare has neither cave nor burrow.
The open field is its home and both
adults and young are well adapted
to it.

A female Nubian ibex, viewed from an unusual angle because it is tame. In the wild an ibex will never allow itself to be looked down on from above.

circumspect and cautious; apparently it reserves its black and white striped head exclusively to the view of its closest intimates.

There are several flesh eaters which cannot be classified as carnivores. Let us begin with the smallest of them, the shrews. Anyone lifting up a rotting sack or moving a pile of rubbish may be surprised to find underneath a tiny, active little creature, very like a mouse but with differently shaped head and body. These little animals never stop eating and in the course of a day consume insects and grubs in excess of their own weight. Another representative of the order Insectivora is the hedgehog (*Erinaceus europaeus*). It spends the day rolled up like a ball, spines pointing outwards, but at night it goes into action, noisily making its way across stones and dead branches. Despite its roly-poly appearance, the hedgehog is a mammal, with a head and four legs like other mammals. Its offspring have no spines when born, though they grow them very quickly. They nurse from their mother in the normal mammalian way. Thanks to its spines, the hedgehog can stand up to larger and more dangerous animals, even snakes.

The largest group of insectivores is the order Chiroptera, bats. Every evening, particularly in summer, the air is filled with their winged bodies as they swoop hither and thither in their tireless pursuit of insects. The layman can only distinguish between the insect eaters on the one hand and the great fruit bat (*Rousettus*), which subsists on fruit, on the other. This last-named pest can descend in its thousands on a fruit orchard and in a single night devour a good part of the season's crop.

While Israel cannot boast the abundance of mammals that may be found in such places as East Africa, it does offer a wide and interesting variety.

'...Get you up this way southward, and go up into the mountain: and see the land, what it is...'

(Numbers 13:17–18)

The blossom of the pomegranate is as red as its fruits, and hints at the pleasures to come.

UNTO A LAND THAT I WILL SHOW THEE

Anyone laying down a book which spares no adjectives in describing the charms and attractions of a particular country is bound to be left with some reservations. He can be sure that the author has not made up all that he writes about, but though there may really be a lizard such as he describes it is only rarely that it emerges from its hole and, even though a certain flower is there to be found, he knows that it only blooms near the top of a certain mountain, and then only for one week in mid-January. Many are the tourists who leave the country disappointed, because they have not even caught a glimpse of all the wonderful things set out in the travel brochures. It is better that the traveller should be armed against possible disappointment and directed to those things which he will certainly be able to see with his own eyes.

What can the reader hope to see if he comes to Israel for a few days or a few weeks, or what may he hope to come across? The tourist who comes for a brief sight-seeing trip or a quick visit to the holy places has little need to worry about the weather. Apart from a few days of heavy rain between December and March and some oppressively hot *sharav* days during April and June, he can move freely out of doors whenever he likes, and if a heavy downpour should chance to drive him away from Jerusalem he can easily go down to Eilat and wander along the beach there in a bathing suit. So much is true for every visitor, but if he is interested in what nature has to offer, or wants to see something special, he would be well-advised to pick his time to match his taste, whether it be for flowers, the nesting season, migratory birds or herds of gazelle or ibex. There is a time and a place for each of these.

What are the principal attractions for the tourist who is interested in natural history, and particularly for the one who wants to look at the countryside through the eyes of the Bible? After mentioning some general phenomena, we will run through the months of the year, noting whatever may be special to each month in the calendar of nature.

Israelis talk a lot about the conquest of the desert and foreigners, too, become impressed by this concept. Yet, far from being conquered, the desert is, and will probably remain, the most attractive element which the country has to offer to a visitor from a more urban society. Here he gets a whiff of something primeval, coming face to face with the forces of nature without the moderating influence of soil, water, trees and dwellings. You need wide-awake senses, and sometimes a good guide, to find your way to the soul of the wilderness; but the soul is there.

Passable roads penetrate into every corner of the desert, yet only a few steps off the highway one feels completely cut off from civilization. The landscape itself is interesting enough, with its fantastic contours, its rocks of different colours, and the changing hues that herald the rising or the setting of the sun. Against this desert background every living thing, both plant and animal, is a model of a different way of accommodating to the difficult conditions.

The Bible cannot be fully understood without absorbing something of the atmosphere of the desert; and this is a comment not limited to the story of the Exodus. The Book of Job, for example, bears throughout its length the mark of life on the periphery of the desert, while the Prophet Jeremiah, who was born and raised in the village of Anatot on the edge of the Judean Desert, used metaphors which reveal their full meaning only to those who take into account the environment to which they refer. Anyone who walks through the red gorges near the copper mines north of Eilat, and then opens Chapter 28 of the Book of Job, will immediately place the writer's source of inspiration: 'There is a path which no fowl knoweth, and which the vulture's eye hath not seen: the lion's whelps have not trodden it, nor the fierce lion passed by it. He putteth his hand upon the rock; he overturneth the mountains by the roots.' And while looking out over the desert from Anatot one hears anew the words of Jeremiah: 'Oh that I had in the wilderness a lodging place of wayfaring men . . .' (Jeremiah 9: 2).

Then there are the wild flowers of March and April. Every country has its wild flowers, but few other places can boast such abundance and variety. Hundreds of different species concentrate their flowering into the short spring season, painting the entire landscape from a rich palette. For flowers, too, we must recommend the desert, where the fresh bright blooms are in such vivid contrast to the rocky, sandy waste lying all about. This is not to say that the hills and plains of the north are lacking in a wealth of beautiful flowers. The bright yellow of the chrysanthemum, the crimson

The bead tree (Melia azedarach), *a native of the Himalayan region, is naturalized in Israel and a popular deciduous tree in many gardens.*

of the poppies, and the shyer varieties growing in the woodland shade, are all worth a visit and are not difficult of access.

In the animal kingdom, we have already described some of the rich variety of birds to be found and hinted at a vast field of operations for the bird-watcher. Some of the water birds of England and the continent of Europe, for example, winter in Israel and an encounter with an old friend from home at an unfamiliar season can be of special interest. During the great migratory seasons, from September to November and again from March to May, enormous flocks of storks or pelicans can be seen on the wing, or resting on the ground, not to mention the flights of smaller migratory birds. Many species of resident birds are completely unknown to people coming from the north, the graceful warbler and the African or common bulbul (*Picnonotus capensis*) to mention only two. Here, the bird-watcher can observe them in his own garden. During the winter, there are large concentrations of scores of different kinds of water birds in the Hula nature reserve and at Ma'agan Michael, or perched along the fishponds in the Beth Shean Valley. In the nesting season, from February until the end of June, experienced bird-watchers can catch glimpses of the nesting and hatching of such varied species as the griffon vulture (*Gyps fulvus*) and the tiny Palestine sunbird (*Cinnyris osea osea*).

For those who like lizards but are pressed for time, it will be possible to see many of the species in the country during the course of normal sight-seeing. It is just a matter of finding the right spot and having the patience to turn over enough stones.

As for the larger mammals, it is possible to be sure of seeing at least three of the more interesting diurnals: the gazelle, the Nubian ibex and the cony. In the hills of Issachar, in south-east Galilee, there are herds numbering several hundred gazelles whose every movement can be observed from a reasonable distance. Smaller herds can also be seen in other parts of the country. It is a thrilling experience to come upon a herd of gazelle grazing at the roadside: the bucks, with their handsome horns, the does and their fawns, face you for a moment as they graze and then, with a swish, flash their neat white rumps in your face and make off with a twitch of their tails.

To be sure of seeing the ibex in summer you should visit the nature reserve at Ein Gedi, or prowl around the hinterland of Eilat for a while. Sheltered by the nature protection laws, the herds are becoming less and less shy as they grow larger and more secure. They go to their water holes at certain hours of the day and they can be met at these points almost without fail at their regular times.

The conies live in small groups, not wandering far from their mountain crevices, and anyone who knows where to look should have little trouble in seeing them. Encounters with other animals, such as wild boars, foxes, hares, wild cats and the like, can be much rarer and a sight of them is more dependent on chance, though certainly not impossible.

above: *Apricot blossom; unlike almond blossom, whose praises are sung by the poets as a symbol of spring, it is no less beautiful.*

above right: *The broom-rape, a handsome parasite, nourishes itself upon the roots of a broom or other bush, and puts forth tall spikes of flowers in spring, without a single green leaf.*

opposite above: *The prickly pear has given its name, sabra, to native-born Jews, because of the sweetness of its fruits, belying its prickly exterior.*

opposite below: *'For their vine is the vine of Sodom', says Deuteronomy, and this bush, growing along the shore of the Dead Sea, is so called, for its fruits deceive by their beauty; inside is no flesh but only silk-tailed seeds.*

above: *The rocky shore south of Rosh Hanikra is unlike any other part of the coast of Israel. The high cliff looks out over coastline and sea and the nooks and crannies are full of marine life, while birds nest in the tiny islands at its foot.*

right: *The cactus family is a newcomer to Israel, with no relatives amongst the native flora. The huge flowers of the cereus open at midnight, attracting the ministrations of many insects.*

Ram pond, Fiala of the ancients, at the foot of Mount Hermon. A jewel in the landscape, geologists may discuss its origin but the sheep are unconcerned.

A modest shower, by northern standards, is enough to cause a flood in the long Paran Valley in the Negev. A wide river will flow here for a few hours and then disappear, leaving only the shining wet river bed.

Moving on from our general observations we come now to our calendar of what is to be seen and when. We will start with October, the time of the Jewish New Year (*Rosh Hashanna*), which heralds the beginning of the year in nature in this part of the world. Passing over the domestic varieties we will confine our guide to wild flowers and animals.

OCTOBER: The skies are a harbinger of the change in seasons. The clouds swell and the sunsets provide breathtaking displays of colour and motion. The first rain, the *yoreh*, is due, and with it comes a sharp change in the weather. The wild fruits are ripening. Some of them are edible, like the wild pears and the hawthorn, and others just decorative, like the red arbutus and the violet-blue phillyrea (*Phillyrea angustifolia*). The bramble (*Rubus*), which bears its fruit along the banks of streams, joins the throng. Bulbs and corms begin to sprout, partly in deference to the rain and partly in response to their own internal rhythms. Spafford's *Sternbergia*, with its orange flowers, bursts forth on the hills of Galilee and in several places in the Negev, accompanied by several varieties of colchicum and crocus.

The bird migration southward grows in strength, bringing vast flocks of storks and here and there a solitary golden oriole (*Oriolus oriolus*). The winter birds arrive and disperse amongst stretches of inland water. Small herds of gazelle, each consisting of a buck and a few does, or else a group of bucks together, may be seen grazing.

NOVEMBER: The rains have come, setting the wild grass to sprouting. The vanguard of the winter flowers, the common narcissus, the cyclamen and the winter crocus, appear upon the scene. The migratory birds are still on the move. The smaller varieties have displaced the larger ones on the banks of the fishponds and the wild ducks, coots (*Fulica atra*) and several species of heron have moved on to the surface of the water. Lapwings (*Vanellus vanellus*) can be seen picking their way across the fragrant fields, while white wagtails (*Motacilla alba*) and robins (*Erithacus rubecula*) make themselves at home in gardens and farmyards.

DECEMBER: The world turns green as the rains become more frequent. Some of the deciduous woodland trees begin to shed their leaves, though the change is hardly noticeable at first. Narcissus and cyclamen are in their prime, and the mandrakes join them in the meadows. Mushrooms, some of them edible, begin to appear beneath the dripping boughs of trees.

The bird population becomes stabilized. The amphibians begin to be active. An incessant croaking accompanies the toads, bound for the water to lay their eggs. Newts appear in rainwater puddles in the coastal plain, and salamanders on Mount Meron and the Carmel range. In the Issachar hills, large herds of gazelle graze on the fresh green grass. The nights are full of fruit bats, come to feed on the berries of the bead tree (*Melia azedarach*).

JANUARY: By now, the cold has slowed down plant activity, though without affecting the development of bulbous plants. The anemone shows its face all over the country in red, white and purple. The yellow ficaria-like buttercup (*Ranunculus ficaria*) and the blue vartan iris begin to bloom. The deciduous trees shed the last of their leaves.

The rarer winter birds — greater flamingoes (*Phoenicopterus ruber*), black storks (*Ciconia nigra*) and cranes (*Grus grus*) — begin to settle down on the ponds and near the Kishon Lake in the Jezreel Valley. Flocks of starlings (*Sturnus vulgaris*) blacken the sky and the fields, congregating in their strange fashion in vast multitudes to roost in the Jordan Valley. The mammals grow their winter coats.

FEBRUARY: The air warms up, and the grass grows more lush. The anemones come into full flower in unbelievable profusion. They are joined by several kinds of iris in the north and in the south, and in Galilee the pastel blue hyacinth scents the air with its sweet smell. The Judas tree begins to show its pink blossom, forerunner of the flowering trees and shrubs. The Negev and the desert begin to bloom, led by the white broom, which spills its flowers over the sands along the coastline too.

left: *Summer is ending and the fields await the rains; meanwhile they make a pleasant place for a stroll.*

right: *The Palestine sunbird is tiny and very beautiful. The male is a gleaming blue-black, the female grey. Here the young chick looks out on the world from its basket-like nest.*

below: *The Ile de Graye, a small rocky island in the Red Sea not far from Eilat, famous in the time of the Crusaders, was a fortress and harbour centuries earlier. Today it is popular with tourists.*

Birds great and small, from the vulture to the graceful warbler and the tit, begin to sit on their nests. The Palestine sunbird chooses a garden for its courtship and nesting, preferring one with large red flowers from which it sucks the nectar. Some of the songbirds have already staked out their domains, proclaiming their title in continuous melody. In the fields you can trace the underground runs of the mole rats (*Spalax*) by the small mounds which they leave on the surface, all leading to a large central mound beneath which is the nest.

MARCH: The flowering of the Negev is at its peak, the prize going to the iris and the tulip. In the northern Negev, whole tracts are bright yellow with dandelion, while stock and mallow and other flowers bloom in abundance. This is the ideal month to ramble in the Negev.

In the north the woodlands begin to stir. The oak and the terebinth deck themselves out in green and red, while the Judas tree, the styrax and the arbutus are in full blossom. At their feet the rich forest undergrowth comes to life, with orchids, iris, tulips, lupin and fritillary.

The first of the new-born mammals begin to move around, and nesting is in full swing among the birds. The birds of prey have begun to sit on their eggs while whole colonies of herons are raising their chicks. The spring migrations begin, and there is a conspicuous change in the composition of the bird population.

272

Wild swans are rare, but tame ones settle down
well, like these three on the waters of Nahal Amal
in the heat of the Beth Shean Valley.

APRIL: The vegetation of the Negev and the desert is now past its prime and the north of the country is at its most colourful. The woods are all in leaf and flower. The early blossoming of March is continued by the rock-rose and the trees of the rose family. The mountain streams strain their banks. There is a rich flowering everywhere: orchids, several kinds of iris and buttercups abound, and whole areas are covered with flowering annuals from the mustard and the composite families.

The bird world is no less active, with the spring migration northward in full swing. Again we see the giant flocks of storks and along the Great Rift, in the Arava, the movements of the birds of prey. The oriole and the nightingale (*Luscinia megarhynchos*) are followed by the summer birds, the short-toed eagle, the turtle dove, the rufous warbler (*Erythropygia galactotes*) and the roller (*Coracias garrulus*). Scores of species are nesting at this time: the songbirds, the white-fronted king-fisher (*Halcyon smyrnensis*) and the hoopoe (*Upupa epops*), which make their nests in the dry earth of steep banks along the water's edge, or even at the roadside, and, amongst ground birds, the rock partridge (*Alectoris graeca*) and the francolin (*Francolinus francolinus*).

This is the season when most mammals whelp: the wild boar, gazelles, ibex, hares and conies. Gazelle fawns can be seen timidly picking their way about, never very far away from their mothers. In the mountain springs in Galilee we can watch the metamorphosis from tadpole to salamander. Now is the best month to tour the northern parts of the country.

MAY: The weather turns warmer, and the flowers go to seed. Such flowers as are left can be found mostly in the woods; snapdragons (*Antirrhinum*), michauxia, madonna lily and climbers. There is an abundance of crimson poppies and purple thistles.

This is the nesting time for the Dead Sea sparrow and the summer birds. The songbirds make good any losses from their first brood and begin their second nesting period. The broods of birds living near water, the moorhen, the spur-winged plover and the stilt, and also the desert partridge (*Ammoperdix heyi*), francolin and rock partridge, hatch out and leave their nests. Gazelles, ibex and conies are trailed by their young as they move about.

JUNE: Nature settles down to two months of relative quiescence. As the spring flowers wither, summer flowers come into bloom. The well-watered areas become more active: in the Hula, the papyrus waves above the swamp and white and yellow water lilies display their charms. Along the mountain streams, the oleanders flower in many shades of pink. The fruits of the Christ-thorn ripen. Songbirds are nesting for the second time while pratincole, tern and plover sit on their eggs on the ground, and the turtle doves nest in the trees above.

The fruit of the carob tree, source of food for the poor man in Jewish folklore, also appears in the Christian tradition, as 'St John's Bread', eaten by St John the Baptist in the wilderness.

right: *This pillar,* amud *in Hebrew, standing at the entrance to the gorge, gives its name to the river which flows through it, Nahal Amud.*

Tiny red berries on a hawthorn, one of the few wild trees to bear edible fruit.

JULY: In this month the blossoming of the water and seashore flowers, and especially the sea daffodil, is at its height. In the Negev the acacia comes into bloom. The sebestena trees at Ein Gedi are covered with red fruit. The sea turtles make their annual journeys up the beaches and the lizards are in full activity.

AUGUST: Flowers are now confined chiefly to the seashore and the areas close to water. The autumn bird migration is about to begin, and the first flocks of storks make their appearance. The dwarf kingfisher and the smaller water birds can be seen along the banks of the fishponds.

SEPTEMBER: The heat of summer begins to wane, and nature starts emerging from its lethargy. Clouds appear towards evening, and sunsets become more colourful. The flowers of the seashore and the water's edge begin to go to seed, and the floral harbingers of the coming season appear: the tall slender stems of the sea squill. Near stretches of water tall reeds wave their silvery plumes above the cat-tails. The southward migration of birds increases and large flocks of storks can be seen once more. Winter birds begin to congregate near ponds. The last chicks emerge from the egg. In gazelle country, in the Issacher hills and elsewhere, the bucks engage in single combat for the favours of the doe.

The year has come full circle.